Addressing Postmodernity

STUDIES IN RHETORIC AND COMMUNICATION
General Editors:
E. Culpepper Clark
Raymie E. McKerrow
David Zarefsky

Barbara A. Biesecker

Addressing Postmodernity
Kenneth Burke, Rhetoric, and
a Theory of Social Change

The University of Alabama Press   Tuscaloosa and London

Library of Congress Cataloging-in-Publication Data

Biesecker, Barbara A.
    Addressing postmodernity : Kenneth Burke, rhetoric, and a theory
of social change / Barbara A. Biesecker.
        p. cm. — (Studies in rhetoric and communication)
    Includes bibliographical references (p.) and index
    ISBN 0-8173-0874-1 (cloth : alk. paper)
        1. Burke, Kenneth, 1897– . 2. Postmodernism (Literature)
3. Rhetoric. 4. Literature and society. 5. Literature,
Modern—20th century—History and criticism. I. Title.
II. Series.
PN98.P67B54 1997
809′.9113—dc21   96-51508

British Library Cataloguing-in-Publication Data available

This book is dedicated to
Trevor Melia,
in gratitude for his quiet wisdom
and timely promptings.

Contents

Acknowledgments

To finish a project such as this and then to reflect upon the conditions of its possibility is to realize that there is nothing further from the truth than the commonly held belief that writing is a solitary affair. For without the instruction, encouragement, assistance, and kindness of a great many people over the past several years this book would never have gone to press. Thus I want to thank my two teachers, Gayatri Chakravorty Spivak, whose life and work continue to orient my being and guide my thinking to this day, and Trevor Melia, for his support and generosity in the early years and his trust in my ability to find my own way in those that followed. I would also like to acknowledge those colleagues, graduate students, and friends at the University of Iowa and the University of Pittsburgh who were helpful in various ways (sometimes unbeknownst to them) as I was struggling to finish this manuscript during a most difficult time: Fred Antzack, Ben Attias, Kendall Bartch, Dieter Boxmann, David Cheshire, Sharon Crowley, Melissa Friedling, Tom Kane, Wade Kenney, John Lyne, Jane Martin, Gerald Mast, Michael C. McGee, Jan Norton, Takis Poulakos, Doug Trank, and Steve Whitson. Special thanks go, once again, to Jan Norton as well as to Marilyn Bordwell, Diane Crosby, and Kerry Johnson for their careful editorial and research assistance. I also want to express my appreciation to Raymie McKerrow, who first encouraged me to submit the manuscript to The University of Alabama Press; to the press's then–head acquisitions editor Nicole Mitchell whose letters and phone calls oftentimes convinced me the task could indeed be done; and to the two still-anonymous readers of my original manuscript whose suggestions for revision had a decisive influence on the final product. I owe an exorbitant debt to James P. McDaniel both for the spirited conversations without which the last chapter of this book would have never been written and for the friendship that, at crucial moments, helped me to bear the whole Dionysian load. Finally, my heartfelt thanks go to Susan Biesecker-Mast for having seen me through from beginning to end and for always having made available to me (oftentimes at the expense of her own comfort) a safe place in which I could think, write, and dream at each step along the way.

Nearly all the chapters of this book have been presented at regional, national, and international conferences or colloquia. Thus for having made it possible for me to "go public" with my work and, hence, benefit from the many exchanges that are the real gift of such events, I must thank: The Speech Communication Association (and, most particularly, The Kenneth Burke Society for having invited KB to respond to the panel on which I was presenting my work), The Summer Institute on Culture and Society, The Rhetoric Society of America, and the Southern Branch of The Kenneth Burke Society (especially David Cratis Williams, who, in organizing a special panel on Kenneth Burke's ontology and epistemology, set the scene for a conversation with James Chesebro that vastly enriched my understanding of dramatism). I also gratefully acknowledge the Office of the Provost at the University of Iowa for a Faculty Development Leave during the fall term of the 1994–95 academic year that made it possible for me to craft the final chapter of this book.

Finally, I thank those publishers and authors who generously gave permission to me to quote extensively from their works:

Excerpts from *Criticism and Social Change* by Frank Lentricchia, copyright © 1983 by the University of Chicago Press;

Excerpts from *Norms of Rhetorical Culture* by Thomas B. Farrell, copyright © 1993 by Yale University Press;

Excerpts from *The Critical Theory of Jürgen Habermas* by Thomas McCarthy, copyright © 1978 by MIT Press;

Excerpts from "Kenneth Burke's *Grammar of Motives:* Speculations on the Politics of Interpretation" by Barbara Biesecker, in *Rhetoric and Ideology: Compositions and Criticisms of Power,* RSA Conference Proceedings, 1989;

Excerpts from *A Grammar of Motives* (1962), *A Rhetoric of Motives* (1962), *The Rhetoric of Religion: Studies in Logology* (1961), and *Language as Symbolic Action: Essays on Life, Literature, and Method* (1966) by Kenneth Burke, used by permission of the University of California Press.

Addressing Postmodernity

1

Entering the Fray

As its title suggests, this book aims to offer an answer to the question, What are the conditions of possibility for social change in postmodernity? Hence, this book moves from the assumption that prior theorizations of social relations and their transformation no longer serve, that the peculiarities and particularities of our postmodern condition necessitate a new conceptualization of the relation of structure and subject. This book is, then, resolutely rhetorical in the rather classical or old-fashioned sense of the term: it is an address to theorists and critics that seeks to redress postmodernity or, at least, one particularly salient feature of it—the fragmentation of the contemporary lifeworld.

This book is rhetorical in another sense as well. It insists on, indeed argues strongly on behalf of, the power of persuasive discourse to constitute audiences out of individuals, to transform singularities into collectivities, to fashion a "we" out of a plurality of "I's," and to move them to collective action. It is, of course, no mere irony that the fragmentation of the contemporary lifeworld that has motivated me to raise again the question of social change seems also to mitigate against my positing rhetorical invention and intervention as an answer to it. That is to say, understood as a condition beset by fragmentation, disidentification, and dissensus, postmodernity seems to bear witness to the utter ineffectuality of rhetoric; the proliferation of difference understood as irreducible heterogeneity that is constitutive of our contemporary lifeworld appears to foreclose the very possibility of anything other than an individualistic or atomistic theory of social change.

However, it is not only the tension between the need for a retheorization of collective social change and the real-lived circumstances that at once seem to announce the necessity of this need and register its impossibility that vexes my project from the start. The task of this book is made ever more difficult by its being written in the wake of poststructuralism, a more or less coherent body of thought that has effected a virtual crisis in the human sciences by calling into question the metaphysical underpinnings that had until the late sixties founded modern social theory and practice. Indeed, whether cast in terms of the death of the author, the critique of the metaphysics of presence, or the deconstruction of identity and the self-same, the thoroughgoing poststructuralist interrogation of our inherited conceptions of being, knowing, and doing on the part of Roland Barthes, Jacques Lacan, Michel Foucault, Jean-François Lyotard, and Jacques Derrida, among others, has resolutely transformed our very relation to the question of social change. To state the matter all too summarily perhaps, the demise of foundations, not the least of which was the sovereign rational subject of Enlightenment philosophy that served as a point of departure for a whole host of theories of emancipation, seems to have left us without any conceptual foothold whatsoever from which to begin.

It is not just interesting but crucial to notice that the challenges postmodernity and poststructuralism pose to a retheorization of social change are deeply related. To be sure, as many leftist explanations assert, history was on the side of the poststructuralists. At least in part, the relative failure of student, civil rights, feminist, and other various countercultural movements to produce major political revolutions in western Europe and the United States during the 1960s drove many human scientists to distrust Enlightenment ideals and their philosophical underpinnings. Furthermore, a rising generation of intellectuals trained during the seventies and prodded by the concrete experiences of their age were perhaps less easily persuaded that the problems of their day could be solved within the framework of Enlightenment concepts. Finding themselves caught within a real-lived contradiction—between living in a society of abundance that "has not abolished hunger . . . while it ha[s] widened the gap between industrial and developing nations, exporting misery and military violence" (Habermas 1970a, 25)—these students began looking for alternative theorizations of the subject in history and society and began finding them in the probings of leading French poststructuralist philosophers.

If, however, as Perry Anderson has so deftly demonstrated in his seminal work *In the Tracks of Historical Materialism*, the post-structuralist interrogation of the subject and the concomitant erosion of Enlightenment ideals drew their inspiration from a socio-historical moment of economic and political malaise, they found their philosophical justification in a whole host of the human sciences' most treasured and canonical works, not the least of which for Anderson were Marx's own. He writes:

[T]he passage from Marxist to structuralist and then post-structuralist dominants in post-war French culture has not involved a complete discontinuity of issues or questions. On the contrary, it is clear that there has been one master-problem around which *all* contenders have revolved; and it would look as if it was precisely the superiority of—in the first instance—structuralism on *the very terrain* of Marxism itself that assured it of decisive victory over the latter. What was this problem? Essentially, the nature of the relationships between structure and subject in human history and society. Now, the enigma of the respective status and position of these two was not a marginal or local area of uncertainty in Marxist theory. Indeed, it has always constituted one of the most central and fundamental problems of historical materialism as an account of the development of human civilization. (33–34)

For practitioners committed to Anderson's own project, the operative rhetorical gesture here insinuates itself between two dashes, as a pause: if it is "in the first instance" that structuralism and, later, poststructuralism appear uniquely capable of accounting for the development of civilization, then it is in "the last instance" that historical materialism will provide theoretical and political guidance. Whether or not historical materialism can make good on its promissory note remains to be seen. However, what cannot go unnoticed is that, even as enterprising leftist intellectuals remain firmly committed to and actively engaged in the project of discerning effective strategies for the dislodgment of oppressive social structures, they are now obliged to do so from the other side of difference. That is to say, a significant proportion of leftist intellectuals have conceded, albeit reluctantly, that deliberate and self-proximate subjects of knowledge and action can no longer found the elaboration of a theory of the distinctive dynamics of social development. The problem now, of course, is to articulate the relations of structure and subject otherwise without eclipsing the radical-critical edge of historical materialism.

In the wake of Saussurean and post-Saussurean linguistics, it is with an eye to language that radical theorists have begun to critique, revise, and reformulate their understanding of social relations and the agents who constitute and are constituted by them. It is not without consequence, however, that the heightened sensitivity to language has not been coupled with an increased attention to rhetoric. It is remarkable indeed that rhetoric, understood as the art of persuasion, is rarely even mentioned by those theorists and critics most preoccupied with social transformation.[1] Though much has been made lately of the symbolic or cultural realms and though volume upon volume has been written about strategies, tactics, and discursive practices, embarrassingly few studies are informed by the lessons of a discipline whose central preoccupation has been to come to terms with the persuasive aspects of symbolic forms.

That most radical theorists and critics have taken a decisive linguistic turn but have failed to even nod in the direction of rhetoric may, of course, be explained by the simple fact that they were trained for the most part in literary theory. Within this tradition, Aristotle's *Poetics* was studied and not his *Rhetoric*; it was in great prose and poetry and not in deliberative, forensic, or epideictic oratory that the conditions of possibility for social and cultural transformation were thought to have been encoded. Moreover, it may be argued that rhetoric has no place when one begins, as these theorists and critics do, to entertain seriously a notion of ideology as something bigger than individual consciousness and will, particularly within a post-structuralist frame. If the subject can no longer be taken as the origin, center, end, reference, evidence, and arbiter of analysis, theory, and practice, and if ideology is the structure through which alternative forms of subjectivity and sociality are effected, then an Aristotelian or neo-Aristotelian conception of rhetoric as a force capable of re-shaping society in accordance with the needs and desires voiced by a given subject on behalf of a particular constituency seems little more than naive optimism. If the speaking subject and the audience are always already, to borrow a rather ostentatious phrase, interpellated by ideology, then the very notion that an individual's deliberate and hortatory use of speech and other symbolic forms can inaugurate collective and counterhegemonic action is itself overdetermined from the start. As Louis Althusser puts it in his now famous essay "Ideology and Ideological State Apparatuses (Notes Towards an Investigation)," "[W]hat thus seems to take place outside ideology (to be precise, in the street), in reality takes place in ideology. What really takes place in ideology seems therefore to take place outside it. That is why those who are in ideology believe themselves by definition outside ideology: one of the effects of ideology is the practical *denegation* of the ideological character of ideology by ideology: ideology never says, 'I am ideological' " (175). Within the perspective of Althusser's structural functionalism, *"ideology is eternal,* exactly like the unconscious" (161) and, thus, rhetoric understood as a speech act authored by freely choosing and acting individuals is theoretically and historically implausible.

Because Althusser's totalizing view of ideology appears to liquidate any role for human agency, radical theorists and critics have begun to look elsewhere for a theory of the dynamic relations of structure and subject. In this effort, it is to the work of Antonio Gramsci that a great many leftist intellectuals have turned. Unlike Althusser, the more tradition-bound leftists argue, Gramsci offers an explanatory model that admits the formidable role of material forces in the production and reproduction of subjects without falling into mechanical determinism and without reinstalling the sovereign subject of Enlightenment philosophy. On the one hand, Gramsci affirms human agency by conceiving history as a continuous and contradictory process that proceeds not from "laws of economic development" alone but, instead or at least in part, from "current relations of force." In fact, for Gramsci, as Patrick Brantlinger puts it, ideology is not "a structuralist abstraction somehow separated from human intentions and practices" (95). Human struggle and negotiation are at the very heart of ideological or, more properly, hegemonic practices through which domination is provisionally achieved. On the other hand, even as Gramsci preserves human agency by refusing to grant the social relations of production absolute and distinct priority, he does not restore the sovereign subject of history. To be sure, human beings act within and upon the social. Nevertheless social interactions, like ideology, are not "willed" or "rational" in the old sense of the terms since, as Stuart Hall cogently puts it, they are "connective across different positions, between apparently dissimilar, sometimes contradictory, ideas." Their " 'unity' is always in quotation marks and always complex, a suturing together of elements which have no necessary or eternal 'belongingness' " (10).

Without a doubt, the more recent post-Marxism evidences the desire to exploit Gramsci's work for a thoroughly nonessentialist theory of social transformation that recognizes domination as an effect of perpetual contestation rather than as something automatically handed over by the class structure. As I noted above, for Stuart Hall, Stanley Aronowitz, Cornel West, and others who stick closer to the concept of class as developed by Marx, the Gramscian viewpoint is understood to make it possible to acknowledge both the discursive character of the process of formation and the conditions of existence that constrain the process of formation itself. For post-Marxists like Ernesto Laclau and Chantal Mouffe, however, Gramsci provides the theoretical conditions for what A. Belden Fields calls the " 'everything social is discourse' approach" (151) in which the irreducibly metaphorical and imperfectly sutured nature of all social practices and identities is not only affirmed but, moreover, posited as the very resource for social change:

> Society as a sutured space, as the underlying mechanism that gives reasons for or explains its own partial processes, does not exist, because if it did, meaning would be fixed in a variety of ways. Society is an ultimate impossibility, an impossible object; and it exists only as the attempt to constitute that impossible object or order. . . . Neither the difference nor the space can be ultimately sutured. We can speak about the logic of the social, but we cannot speak of society as an ultimately rational and intelligible object. And the fact that we cannot speak of society in such a way is why we have to have a concept of hegemonic relations. Hegemonic relations depend upon the fact that the meaning of each element in a social system is not definitely fixed. If it were fixed, it would be impossible to rearticulate it in a different way, and thus rearticulation could only be thought under such categories as false consciousness. (Laclau 1988, 254)

For Laclau and Mouffe social change takes place because each element in the always already open system has a surplus of meaning that cannot be totally absorbed by the system. As they argue in their book, *Hegemony and Socialist Strategy: Towards a Radical Democratic Politics*, the surplus or excess that marks the failure of absolute identity is the potential reserve of social conflict or antagonism that manifests itself as political struggle within a vast textual chain.

Despite the profound differences between the highly controversial post-Marxism of Laclau and Mouffe and the more moderate neo-Gramscian approach, what each side has in common is, as I noted above, a general refusal to theorize the role of rhetoric in the process of social transformation. Upon first glance Laclau and Mouffe, rather than the neo-Gramscians, seem closest to claiming rhetoric as a vital component of any possible emancipatory project. However, in marshalling a particular interpretation of French poststructuralism in order to propose a paradigm of social change that exposes the essentialism inherent in historical materialism, Laclau and Mouffe's work operationalizes a notion of rhetoric-as-figuration that displaces not only the world-historical agent but also the art of persuasion. Here rhetoric is neither more nor less than the name for the unwitting and discursively constituted excess that escapes structure.

Oddly enough, however, it is in work of the neo-Gramscians that the absence and need of a theory of rhetoric are felt the most. Indeed, it is precisely at those moments wherein Hall, for example, seems to be on the verge of addressing the role and status of persuasion in social change that his discourse breaks off. His essay "Gramsci and Us" may serve as one case in point. Having made the argument that Gramsci's work enables us to better understand our contemporary historical conjuncture by obliging us to attend to the specificity and heterogeneity of political practice, he writes, "[Gramsci's notion of a 'historical bloc'] entails a quite different conception of how social forces and movements, in their diversity, can be articulated into a set of strategic alliances. To construct a new cultural order, you need not to reflect an already-formed collective will, but to fashion a new one, to inaugurate a new historic project" (170). Given Hall's proclivity toward and dexterity with theory, it is curious indeed that this two-sentence paragraph that all but announces the passage into rhetoric is followed not by its theoretical elaboration but, instead, by a retreat into a scathing critique of the organized left in Britain. Ironically enough it is the Labour leadership's failure to put into practice what Hall himself leaves untheorized that provokes his admonition.

It should perhaps be stressed that it is not necessary to push deconstructively upon the outer limits of Hall's text in order to find in it a demand for a theory of rhetoric that can, in his particular case, supplement Gramsci's elaboration of hegemony. Hall's own work, like the work of other neo-Gramscians, tacitly situates what I am referring to as the rhetorical enterprise not at the margins but at the very center of his project. Even Perry Anderson's book, to which I referred above, closes with an invocation of rhetoric couched within an encomium of Marxism. In the final paragraph he writes, "Marxism has no reason to abandon its Archimedean vantage-point: the search for subjective agencies capable of effective strategies for the dislodgement of objective structures. But amidst pervasive changes within world capitalism today, those three terms can only be successfully combined if they have a common end that is at once desirable and believable for millions who are now hesitant or indifferent to them" (105–6). For Anderson, as for Hall and a great many other leftist intellectuals, the transformation of the social "has to do, in part, with how to construct the social imaginary in ways which enable us to see ourselves transformed in the mirror of politics, and thus to become its 'new subjects' " (Hall 13). Here is a project that the rhetorical theorist standing in the twilight of subjectivity can understand.

Jürgen Habermas's universal pragmatics is hailed by many social and (most notably given the focus of this particular study) rhetorical theorists and critics as the most promising theorization of the relation of structure and subject to have come down the philosophical pike since the linguistic turn precisely because it takes practical argument as fundamental to the transformation of social relations. Seeking to avoid the theoretical excesses and, thus, political pitfalls that he understands are part and parcel of thoroughly contextual or discursive approaches to contemporary collective life and social change, namely infinite regress and relativism, Habermas proposes a procedural concept of communicative action out of which a collective rational will may emerge. As is well known, Habermas's elaborate theorization of the achievement of consensus in practical discourse or argument, which comes into sharp focus in his conceptualization of the ideal speech situation, aims to save the idea of reason and the rational subject derived from the Enlightenment by transforming it. That is to say, in striking contrast to the theorists discussed above, Habermas argues on behalf of a postmetaphysical universalism that both flies in the face of the circular, closed-off structure of unifying reason and repudiates the celebration of the resolutely contradictory and conflictual that he takes to be at the heart of radical contextualism. Indeed, in championing a conception of reason and the rational subject that unabashedly aims to capitalize on the emancipatory possibilities latent in Enlightenment thought while leaving its metaphysical trappings behind, Habermas demonstrates a theoretical tenacity that, as John Peters has duly noted, is "bound up with his more general *modus operandi* of rescuing the positive moment from political circumstances whose impurity could daunt the more squeamish" (541). This can be accomplished, Habermas claims,

with the transition to a new paradigm, that of mutual understanding (*Verständigung*). Subjects capable of speaking and acting who, against the background of a common lifeworld, come to an understanding with each other about something in the world, relate to the medium of their language both autonomously and dependently: they can make use of grammatical rule-systems which make their practices possible in the first place, for their own purposes as well. Both moments are equiprimordial. On the one hand, these subjects always find themselves already in a linguistically structured and disclosed world; they live off of grammatically projected interconnections of meaning. To this extent, language sets itself off from the speaking subjects as something antecedent and objective, as the structure that forges conditions of possibility. On the other hand, the linguistically disclosed and structured lifeworld finds its footing only in the practices of reaching understanding within a linguistic community. (1992, 43)

While a great deal can be said about this passage, suffice it to say here that Habermas's claim to having articulated a viable postmetaphysical theory of social change hinges on the extent to which his situated concept of understanding or reason and, thus, the formation of consensus that is the intersubjectively produced outcome of communicative exchange truly escape from rather than remain mired in a theory of language that colonizes the potentially radicalizing force of lived speech or rhetoric. That is to say, in developing a nonessentialist theory of the relations of structure and subject that does not simply accommodate or incorporate the art of public deliberation but takes it as the primary means of progressive social transformation, Habermas appears to have already provided the kind of framework that I am claiming has yet to be developed. But as I will argue in the last chapter, appearances can be deceiving.

To be sure, my recapitulation of what many historians are now calling the recent "crisis in the humanities" is not only brief but also singular in its focus. However, I have chosen to feature the left's response to the philosophical assault on humanism not because I wish to set up a straw man argument against which I can then, more persuasively, pitch my own. I have put my emphasis there because, as I hope is obvious by this point, I find in much of the writing done by these contemporary theorists some of the most theoretically useful and practically plausible descriptions to date of the complex processes through which subjectivities are constructed and reconstructed in history. In fact, one way to describe my project in this book is to say that I want to push forward these attempts to refigure the relations between structure and subject within a post-Enlightenment frame by turning back to the work of Kenneth Burke.

Why Burke? Why go back to the work of "this man without tenure, a Ph.D., or even a B.A., who writes books that cannot be touched by conventional academic definition" (Lentricchia 1982, 119)? What possible sense could it make to revisit the writings of a bonafide bricoleur who, over nearly a century, has written poetry, short stories, and a novel, has composed music and orchestrated translations, has criticized the arts and its critics, and has crafted literary, rhetorical, and social theory? To all of these questions, which are rhetorical not because they have no answer, but because they have more than one answer and, thus, to choose one is to displace the many others, I respond: by insisting on the constitutive role of rhetoric in the formation of individual and collective subjects, Burke's work productively supplements contemporary understandings of the relations of structure and subject. Indeed, in the end I want to claim that Burke's work puts us on the track of an alternative theorization of the relations of structure and subject that, in taking rhetoric seriously into account, can admit the role of human agency in the making and unmaking of social structures and history without resurrecting the sovereign subject of Enlightenment philosophy.

Now it should perhaps be said that "new" theoretical ground is rarely, if ever, broken without a bit of subterranean shifting beforehand. Thus it should come as no surprise that my thesis is, if not underwritten by, at least subtended by a rich history of Burkeian criticism: rich to be sure, but tumultuous as well. Indeed, it is worth noticing that the past sixty-five years or so of critical analyses have not produced an incremental series of readings that, strictly speaking, collectively and progressively develop and refine our understanding of Burke's work. Instead, the history of Burkeian scholarship is marked by discontinuity and rupture, statement and counterstatement, proposition and negation. The history of Burkeian scholarship is, in short, riddled by an oftentimes hostile "conflict of interpretations": while some critics will claim Burke's work for Marxism (Lentricchia 1982, 1983, 1989; Bygrave), others will align it with formalism (Jameson 1982; Murray), pluralism (Booth 1974–75, 1979; Crusius), structuralism (Rueckert 1963, 1969b; Donoghue), semiotics (Fiordo; Neild), and even poststructuralism (Freccero; Nelson; Williams). To what do we attribute these incommensurate and competing readings? Are some of these critics simply wrong? Are some of these writings mere "misreadings"? Or is it the case, as William Rueckert has argued in one of his most recent essays, that "[t]he uses of Burke . . . are as many as there are Burkes"; that "[h]e is truly one of our most protean figures, and it would seem that we have, at last, just begun to discover him" (1982, 30)?

However one chooses to answer the question of Burke's allegiance to any particular theoretical "school," Rueckert is surely right when, in his still respectfully cited book, *Kenneth Burke and the Drama of Human Relations* (1963), he asserts that Burke's work has invariably sought to move "beyond language . . . by and through language" (162). It may even be the case that it is precisely concerning this relation between any symbolic act and its more or less adequately specified "outer-space" to which Burke refers that the critical conflict over his work has taken place. To be sure, despite the profound differences among their ultimate placements of Burke, a key problem for almost all of these critics has been what to make of Burke's often-repeated claim that any symbolic action must always be thought of in relation to something external to itself.

In his 1978 article "The Symbolic Inference; or, Kenneth Burke and Ideological Analysis," Fredric Jameson is quite predictably interested in drawing out of Burke's theory and practice the presumed relations of a text and its "social text" so as to discern the serviceability of dramatism for materialist critique and, ultimately, social transformation. It would seem to be the case, Jameson writes, that one can locate a point of departure for ideological analysis in Burke's "conception of the symbolic as act or *praxis*" (70). When interpreted within the context of their production, Burke's early and middle works emerge as "a critique of the more mindless forms of the fetishism of language" characteristic of the day:

Burke's stress on language, far from reinforcing as it does today the ideologies of the intrinsic and of the anti-referential text, had on the contrary the function of restoring to the literary text its value as activity and its meaning as a gesture and a response to a determinate situation. Thus conceived, literary and cultural criticism takes its place among the social sciences, and the study of language and of aesthetic objects in general recovers something of the dignity it had for the founders of philology when their program foresaw the analysis of literary texts and monuments as a unique means of access to the understanding of social relations. (70–71)

According to Jameson, however, Burke's initial inclination to decipher symbolic forms as responses to the social scenes out of which they emerge is outstripped by a set of methodological procedures that tend, "by focusing our attention on the inner mechanisms of the symbolic act in question, to end up bracketing the act itself and to suspend any interrogation of what constitutes it as an act in the first place, namely its social and ideological purpose" (78). On his reading, the protocols of dramatism and, most particularly, Burke's category of purpose "rule out of bounds the very perspective [that the method] began by promising us, namely that vaster social or historical or political horizon in which alone the symbolic function of those symbolic acts which are the verbal and literary artifacts can become visible to us" (78–79).

Jameson's discomfort with Burke's work, however, goes well beyond the argument that dramatism hermetically seals the critic off from what Jameson will call the text's "political unconscious" or the contradictory social conditions that underpin it. Even more crucial to Jameson than the limits dramatism imposes on the practice of literary criticism per se is the political conservatism embedded in the theory of subjectivity that informs it. For Jameson dramatism finishes up as a theory of human action and subjectivity whose investment in the ideology of bourgeois individualism serves to perpetually undermine collective identification and counterinsurgency. "The very figure of the drama," Jameson writes,

is itself in this respect infinitely revealing and infinitely suspect: the theatrical spectacle, theatrical space, indeed furnishes the first and basic model of the mimetic illusion, just as it is the privileged form in which the spectator-subject finds itself assigned a place and a center. Drama is then not so much the archetype of praxis as it is the very source of the ideology of representation and, with it, of the optical illusion of the subject, of that vanishing point from which spectacles—whether of culture, of everyday life, or of history itself—fall into place as metaphysically coherent meanings and organic forms. (88)

The very possibility of the emergence of a collective subject of radical social transformation depends, according to Jameson, at least in part on making painfully visible, rather than covering over, the ideological contradictions of real-lived experience. Thus a theory of symbolic *action* that rests upon a theory of representation that thoroughly absorbs those contradictions finishes up as a theory of *symbolic* action that fails ultimately to affirm the radical possibilities for human intervention into structure.

Curiously enough, in his book-length study *Criticism and Social Change,* Frank Lentricchia finds in Burke's work what Jameson could not: a serious, sustained, and, in the final analysis, successful engagement with the issue of structure and subject that manifests itself as a decisive commitment to human praxis and social change. In fact, Lentricchia's generous reading identifies Burke as a "critical theorist of social change" (31) whose meditations on the interlocking relations constitutive of subjectivity, sociality, and signification oblige critics who would be a social force to rediscover Burke's uncanny contemporaneity. Though Burke uses the traditional term *representation* to stand in for symbolic action in general, it "carries none of the freight that it is generally made to carry in the history of mimetic theories of art" (153). To the contrary, "[s]ymbolic action as 'representation' is an activity simply charged with power, an activity we can call aesthetic praxis provided that we understand the aesthetic against the grain of the highly specialized meaning that tends to dominate thought about literature and art since the late eighteenth century" (153). Pushing the point even further, Lentricchia argues that it is precisely by reading against the grain of a certain history that it becomes possible to "retrieve [in Burke's work] a more classical sense of the aesthetic *as* the practical and *as* the rhetorical: the aesthetic as the sine qua non of the cultural economy" (153).

When situated within the context of the history of Anglo-American Marxist literary criticism and theory, the most exceptional feature of Lentricchia's analysis may be his readiness to struggle with and take into account what most leftist literary theorists and critics refuse even to notice. In comparison with other leftist intellectuals Lentricchia is uniquely willing to entertain the suggestion that rhetoric understood as "any use of language [not excepting the literary] that has the effect of shaping and controlling attitudes and behavior" (103) is integral to the process of social transformation. As he puts it in one of the most astute passages in the book wherein he writes specifically about Burke's address at the first American Writers' Congress: "It is not a question of whether there is a teleology in history—a question for metaphysicians and some Marxists—but a question of forging the rhetorical conditions for change, a question of forging (and I'll insist on the Joycean resonance of that term) of a teleological rhetoric, of creating, through the mediations of such discourse, a collective will for change, for moving history in the direction of our desire" (37). In short, Lentricchia situates the very promise of social revolution squarely within the rhetorical realm rather than positing it as something ultimately assured by the teleological thrust of history. Of the importance of Burke's conception of rhetoric for the ends of social change, Lentricchia unabashedly declares: "[T]he fate of Marxism will be decided by the active involvement of individuals in the great struggle of persuasion. To say this about the fate of socialism, that *it will be decided in rhetorical war*, is to say nothing especially specific to its vision. The fate of all visions, or nightmares, as the case may be, of the good life, will be similarly decided. 'Decided' is too weak: 'chosen' " (163, emphasis added).

Lentricchia is quite right, I think, in reading in Burke's theory of rhetoric a notion of conscious choice and agency. However, the question that remains to be answered is, What assures us that any human being, operating as an individual or as part of a collectivity, can or will *choose*? On what, besides a leap of faith, may we presume that human beings *can* act in the strictest sense of the term? Early in his career, Lentricchia notes, Burke claimed that human beings can deliberately intervene in structure because they are by "nature" capable of action. That is to say, because human beings are operated by an innate "desire for freedom that is 'prior' to history," a mode of being in the world that "is not itself caught up in the conflicts and partialities of interpretation" (58) is always already available to them. Later, in *A Grammar of Motives*, however, Burke advanced a quite different account of the possibility for human action and agency, one that "forecasts the critique of structuralism mounted in the work of Foucault and Derrida" (67) but does not radically annihilate, as does deconstruction, "all humanist desire for the free subject" (72). Indeed, according to Lentricchia, what distinguishes Burke's "deconstruction of the subject-agent" (73) from those deconstructions that would later be generated by Derrida and his progeny is nothing less than the former's refusal to "eliminate all humanist desire for the free subject" (72). Although like Derrida and de Man the Burke of *A Grammar of Motives* refuses to grant special privilege to the autonomous actor-subject, he does so by seeing the agent "as *having* a constraining context" (71). Here I can do no better than to quote Lentricchia at some length:

In his stunning discussion of the "paradox of substance," Burke locates in the term a strange self-difference. Substance differs from itself, for it moves between a sense that denotes what a thing intrinsically is—that part of the thing uniquely there and nowhere else, that makes the thing what it is and confers its special identity—and a sense (etymologically evident) that denotes a thing's support: *sub-stance*, that upon which the thing stands, what is beneath it—its "foundation" (from the Greek: a standing under). The paradox, then, is that "the word 'substance,' used to designate what a thing *is*, derives from a word designating what a thing is *not*. That is, though used to designate something *within* the thing, intrinsic to it, the word etymologically refers to something *outside* the thing, *extrinsic* to it." Or, to sharpen the paradox still further: used ordinarily to refer to the special interior presence of a thing, etymologically the word refers us to a context, again "something that the thing is *not.*" In this strategic terminological moment, when the "intrinsic and extrinsic change places," we confront the bedrock of the "antinomy of definition." It is a perilous kind of bedrock, however, since no secure footing is provided; it is precisely security, in fact, that Burke is doing away with. The concept of substance, the one thing that must not differ from itself if definition is to be definition, is endowed with what Burke calls an "unresolvable ambiguity," but which we can call, after Derrida, "undecidability," since no choice can be made between two very different senses. This perverse playfulness of undecidability, in evidence in Burke's cultivation of the paradoxes of substance and act, is not the despair of history. Rather it is first the very condition of transformation that makes a certain kind of historical consciousness possible; second, it is the condition that opens, once and for all, the autonomous, closed, and unified subject to historical process; Burke deconstructs the subject *in order to* historicize it; and third, by questioning and subverting the fundamental "originating" claim of "action," Burke's dramatistic dance on "action" radically historicizes its significance. With the self-presence of key Western terms like "substance" and "act" so unstabilized by Burke's analysis, we are prepared to confront, in the terminological dimension itself, a more detailed and heterogeneous level of history than we have been accustomed to knowing. (74–75)

Writing in the wake of the critique of Enlightenment philosophies, Lentricchia is a shrewd enough theorist to recognize that what was once considered to be Burke's failure to adhere to a strict Marxian theory of social transformation and its implications for human agency may now be tapped as a strength. Still, a more critical view would call into question the clarity of the lines of difference and points of collaboration Lentricchia traces out between deconstruction and Burkeian dramatism and, thus, ask the theorist to address a less simplified view of the former, if not of the latter as well.

One more point needs to be made about Lentricchia's interpretation of Burke's work. It may not be far from the truth to say that Lentricchia's retrieval of what he calls the "more fundamental Burkeian activity . . . of reading and writing history" (55) is, oddly enough, underwritten by a progressivist narrative taxonomy not altogether unlike Hegel's teleological theory of history. As I have hinted above, Lentricchia emplots Burke's intellectual "development" in terms of a diminution in the self-alienation of the theorist himself; we are, Lentricchia tells us, best able to retrieve the "more fundamental Burkeian activity" when we interpret the earlier work as a step toward a coherent vision. When we come across, as Lentricchia does in *Permanence and Change,* for example, a moment wherein Burke's essentializing strategies would make even the strictest of structuralists proud, we are not to ignore it but, rather, read it as evidence of a mind in the process of enlarging itself since the "real" Burke emerges in *A Grammar of Motives*, a book wherein the two conflicting tendencies that had riddled his thought—a "desire to be systematic" and a desire to resist "the essentializing consequences of systematic thought" (56)—find their resolution in his deconstruction of the subject-agent. One could, of course, object to Lentricchia's interpretation of Burke on the grounds that a constitutive contradiction obtains between the nonteleological theory of history Lentricchia seems to want to advocate via Burke and the quite deterministic and continuist theory of history he operationalizes in order to interpret Burke's work. Be that as it may, given the protocol of reading that informs Lentricchia's interpretation of the Burke corpus, what seems most peculiar about Lentricchia's project is failure to see it to its completion. The authority of the analysis is compromised, radically it seems to me, by his refusal to even mention several of Burke's later writings, especially *The Rhetoric of Religion: Studies in Logology.* In fact, Lentricchia stops reading midway in Burke's career. Thus if Lentricchia is not to throw into question the usefulness of a certain model of history even as he declares it to be the key to understanding Burke's work, it seems to me that his use of the "thirties man" would have to take into account, however briefly, the later work, which, according to a number of critics, at least seems to move away from, if not directly to contradict, what Lentricchia posits as Burke's culminating position.[2]

If I have dwelt long on Lentricchia's analysis it is because I think he tackles, masterfully at times, Burke's persistent attempt to specify the dynamic relations of structure and subject, history and human agency, permanence and change. However, I do not think it accurate (in the old-fashioned sense of the term) or even particularly useful (in the long run) to interpret within a developmental model of history—what Jameson would call a dialectical and utopian hermeneutics—the series of attempts on Burke's part to come to terms with the structure-subject problematic. That is to say, I do not think that the progressivist narrative framework Lentricchia adopts, even if it were filled out, does justice to the precarious character of Burke's thought. To be sure, as more than one critic has already noticed, Burke's writing oftentimes tries the patience of the most virtuous readers among us. I would suggest, however, that this is not because the system is so complex and intricately woven that it resists our attempts to master it. Instead, I would suggest that this is so because Burke's thought is constantly on the move, perpetually on the make, chronically undoing itself. If, as Trevor Melia once said, "one can begin anywhere in Burke," that may be because Burke's works resemble more a crypt than a maze; more the working out of a desire than the accomplishment of a project. All of this is not meant to suggest that I do not see Burke affirming, or negating, as the case may be, distinct positions. It is meant to suggest, however, that the series of decisive engagements we call Burke's thought may not be best understood by assuming that a logic of progression obtains between them.[3] For in presuming progression one becomes obliged, wittingly or not, to discount or sublate the false starts, delays, fissures, and detours that, I want to argue, open up for Burke and for us quite unanticipated theoretical and critical possibilities.

Because I am interested in locating and productively exploiting the unanticipated theoretical and critical possibilities written into Burke's texts, this study will adhere to a deconstructive strategy of reading: one that, attitudinally and procedurally, aims to open, to produce rather than protect, to refuse the absolute authority of the text. The most compact description of the deconstructive project may be a phrase from Derrida's well-known essay "White Mythology." Derrida writes, "The issue is . . . to deconstruct [*deconstruire*] the metaphysical and rhetorical schema which are at work [in the text], not in order to reject and discard them but to reinscribe them otherwise" (215). While there are several points worth noting here, one in particular needs to be underscored: the stress Derrida places on the doubled movement of deconstructive practice. Indeed, what has been almost uniformly overlooked or, at best, given mere lip service by theorists and critics hostile to poststructuralism is that the strategy of reading advanced by Derrida involves two critical gestures rather than just one. In fact, it may not be too far from the truth to suggest that one can attribute the profoundly philosophical ethos of Gayatri Spivak's translator's preface to the *Grammatology* to Spivak's anticipation of a readership anxious to make deconstruction inhabitable by way of its domestication. To be sure, bringing to her reading of Derrida's text (indeed his entire corpus as of that date) an uncommon philosophical rigor and subtlety of hand that permits the different threads and different lines of meaning to circulate, Spivak emphasizes, almost to the point of being redundant, the "doubled" nature of the deconstructive morphology. In a brief recapitulation of a much longer description that precedes, she writes, "To locate the promising marginal text, to disclose the undecidable moment, to pry it loose with the positive lever of the signifier; to reverse the resident hierarchy, only to displace it; to dismantle in order to reconstitute what is always already inscribed. Deconstruction in a nutshell" (lxxvii). Thus in the course of the critique the deconstructor both follows the itinerary of an undoing *and* enunciates, from within that terrain of undecidability, a supplement. That is to say, deconstruction entails a double predication, a two-step that, contrary to intellectual gossip, affirms rather than deplores radical possibility.

But what does that mean? One very good answer may be found on the last page of the *Grammatology* wherein Derrida closes with a note by Rousseau that may be read as an (allegorical) description of deconstructive practice: "[T]he dreams of a bad night are given to us as philosophy. You will say I too am a dreamer; I admit it, but I do what others fail to do, I give my dreams as dreams, and leave the reader to discover whether there is anything in them which may prove useful to those who are awake" (316). But if the dream of the deconstructor is to articulate the supplement, if the desire is to set about the task of rebuilding, how exactly does the critic go about it? To answer this question one can do no better than to turn to an interview conducted by Jean-Louis Houdebine and Guy Scarpetta wherein Derrida tries to spell out the rules of a deconstructive reading. He says:

[Deconstruction] proceed[s] using a double gesture, according to a unity that is both systematic and in and of itself divided, a double writing, that is, a writing that is in and of itself multiple, what I called, in *"La double séance,"* a *double science.* On the other hand, we must traverse a phase of *overturning.* To do justice to this necessity is to recognize that in a classical philosophical opposition we are not dealing with the peaceful coexistence of a *vis-à-vis,* but rather with a violent hierarchy. One of the two terms governs the other (axiologically, logically, etc.), or has the upper hand. To deconstruct the opposition, first of all, is to overturn the hierarchy at a given moment. To overlook this phase of overturning is to forget the conflictual and subordinating structure of opposition. Therefore one might proceed too quickly to a *neutralization* that *in practice* would leave the previous field untouched, leaving one no hold on the previous opposition, thereby preventing any means of *intervening* in the field effectively. We know what always have been the *practical* (particularly *political*) effects of *immediately* jumping *beyond* oppositions, and of protests in the simple form of *neither* this *nor* that. When I say that this phase is necessary, the word *phase* is perhaps not the most rigorous one. It is not a question of a chronological phase, a given moment, or a page that one day simply will be turned, in order to go on to other things. The necessity of this phase is structural; it is the necessity of an interminable analysis: the hierarchy of dual oppositions always reestablishes itself. Unlike those authors whose death does not await their demise, the time for overturning is never a dead letter.

That being said—and on the other hand—to remain in this phase is still to operate on the terrain of and from within the deconstructed system. By means of this double, and precisely stratified, dislodged and dislodging, writing, we must also mark the interval between inversion, which brings low what was high, and the irruptive emergence of a new "concept," a concept that can no longer be, and never could be, included in the previous regime. (41–42)

By attending to the minute details of the text and by following carefully the turns of argument and metaphoric displacements, the deconstructor locates within the text itself a vertiginous moment that utterly challenges the founding assumption that enabled the writing to proceed. In doing so the critic, as Derrida puts it, "make[s] room for 'the irruptive emergence of a new "concept," a concept which no longer allows itself to be understood in terms of the previous regime' " (Spivak 1976, lxxvii). This new "concept" is nothing other than the supplement.

It is in accordance with the rules of deconstructive practice, then, that I shall read Burke's work. Hence I shall refuse to grasp textual discrepancies either as regrettable or repairable errors on an otherwise flawless surface or as signposts of the wholesale and unidirectional movement of an autonomous intending subject. Instead I shall present a reading of Burke's work that will begin by charting the protocols of the texts (the rules by which the game is played), but that will always already be prepared to follow the precarious rule of a textual aporia "which harbors the unbalancing of the equation" (Spivak 1976, xlix). More particularly, I will read three of Burke's texts, *A Grammar of Motives*, *A Rhetoric of Motives*, and *The Rhetoric of Religion: Studies in Logology*, in both a relatively traditional way, paying particular attention to the logical operations of the declared arguments and seeking to produce descriptions of them, and in a relatively nontraditional way, trying to make visible the manner in which those dominant logics begin to unravel from within. Again, however, the deconstruction of Burke's texts will not be motivated by a desire to simply locate and expose an error on Burke's part. Rather, textual discrepancies will be grasped as irreducible moments that move us beyond the declared claims of the particular texts, as critical self-transgressions that put us on the track of something resolutely other, of something that each text only imperfectly postpones—a "new" conception of the relations of structure and subject, of history and rhetoric, which, to borrow the phrase from Derrida once again, "no longer allows itself to be understood in terms of the previous regime" (1976, lxxvii). The dream of the final chapter of this book is, by borrowing the resources of this new conception from the logic it deconstructs and, thus, finding its very foothold there, to specify it.

About the task of this book and the use of a deconstructive strategy of reading in order to accomplish it, two more points must be stated. First, a deconstructive critique does entail a critical gesture. Indeed, though I have tried to stress, for the reasons specified above, the deconstructive "phase" of remaking, there can be no doubt that the project does challenge the authority of the text; that the critic does confront the text with an eye out for its limits. In terms of my reading of Burke, then, all of this means I will move into his writing with the attitude that "this is not it, that is not all." I suspect that such an approach to Burke will not sit well with a great many scholars who will diagnose my approach as a sign of clandestine disrespect for the father of modern rhetoric or perhaps even as a symptom of failure on my part to appreciate the delicate workings of a mind whose capacities far outstrip my own. In anticipation of such charges I simply say that I only demand of Burke what he always demanded of others: that we engage in persistent critique, that we refuse to forget that it is always "more complicated than that" (1970, 277). Indeed, borrowing the words of Louis Dupré on Marx, I would suggest that "[t]he very nature of [Burke's] undertaking excludes uncritical acceptance" and that "[o]ne hardly serves the interests of an oeuvre written against the uncritical use of authority by taking its own authority for granted" (13). Thus I shall choose to read Burke's work in the spirit that it has been given to us: as "equipment for living" and as a discourse whose contemporary efficacy demands we "use" it rather than entomb it, however deferentially. Such is the responsibility, the risk, indeed the burden of the critic whose most precious and precocious wish is to enter into the fray we call history.

Second, given what I have said about the kind of analysis of Burke's work that will be advanced here and, perhaps more important, given the intellectual climate within which the academic now writes, one might object *ab initio* to this study on the grounds that it absolutely fails to explain Burke's work by reference to something else. To this charge I shall only say this: it is true that I have decided to situate myself within the texts themselves, that I will not read the texts in relation to their sociohistorical and cultural contexts, and that I am holding at bay a vast stream of intertextuality (both in its narrow and general sense) of which these texts are certainly a part. If it is to three of Burke's texts and the arguments presented therein that I grant a particular (albeit provisional) privilege, however, that is because I write as someone who believes there is something in them that has yet to be deciphered and that cannot be deciphered if we too quickly find in culture and in history an alibi for our own impatience with the writing.

Perhaps a few words on the texts themselves are in order. As I hope is abundantly clear by now, the aim of this book is to read Burke's work deconstructively for a "new" concept of the dynamic relations of structure and subject and for a "new" theory of social change that takes rhetoric seriously into account. Furthermore, although it may be true that one could "begin anywhere in Burke," I will concentrate on three landmark books: *A Grammar of Motives, A Rhetoric of Motives,* and *The Rhetoric of Religion: Studies in Logology.* The decision to single out these three books finds its justification in the introduction to the *Grammar* wherein Burke reflects in some detail upon the series of events that led him to write what is, properly speaking, his unfinished trilogy of motives. He states:

> In our original plans for this project, we had no notion of writing a "Grammar" at all. We began with a theory of comedy, applied to a treatise on human relations. Feeling that competitive ambition is a drastically over-developed motive in the modern world, we thought this motive might be transcended if men devoted themselves not so much to "excoriating" it as to "appreciating" it. Accordingly, we began taking notes on the foibles and antics of what we tended to think of as "the Human Barnyard."
>
> We sought to formulate the basic stratagems which people employ, in endless variations, and consciously or unconsciously, for the outwitting or cajoling of one another. Since all these devices had a "you and me" quality about them, being "addressed" to some person or to some advantage, we classed them broadly under the heading of a Rhetoric. There were other notes, concerned with modes of expression and appeal in the fine arts, and with purely psychological or psychoanalytic matters. These we classed under the heading of Symbolic.
>
> We had made still further observations, which we at first strove uneasily to class under one or the other of these two heads, but which we were eventually able to distinguish as the makings of a Grammar. For we found in the course of writing that our project needed a grounding in formal considerations logically prior to both the rhetorical and the psychological. And as we proceeded with this introductory groundwork, it kept extending its claims until it had spun itself from an intended few hundred words into nearly 200,000, of which the present book is revision and abridgement. (xix–xx)

In this extraordinarily interesting passage to which I will return more than once, Burke schematically outlines the plans for a new project. *A Grammar of Motives*, he tells us, is the beginning point, the first book in this trilogy of motives. It is to be followed by *A Rhetoric of Motives*, and the *Symbolic* will mark its completion. Now, taking our heuristic cue from Gayatri Spivak (who takes hers from Derrida) and tracking carefully Burke's declarations about the structure of this project, we could make a grammatical allegory of the promised trilogy: Subject (*Grammar*); Copula (*Rhetoric*); Predicate (*Symbolic*). "That would be," Spivak points out, "the structure of the proposition, the irreducible form of the logic of non-contradiction [identity], the simplest and most powerful sentence" (1987, 30–31). Thus I shall read this sentence even though the copula brings trouble and even though the predication goes awry (the *Symbolic of Motives* remains unfinished and another book, *The Rhetoric of Religion*, has come to take its place in this signifying chain). That is to say, I will take this trilogy of a piece even as it performs a copulation other than the one originally intended. Indeed the message of this entire study may find its own allegorical expression in this imperfect predication of Burke's: history and the human beings that shape and are shaped by it do not always, like a language, conform to the demands of a grammar. But then, again, that may be a gift, for inscribed in the "failure" of grammar (here we could substitute structure, dialectic, history) are the radical possibilities of rhetoric.

Finally, I have a brief schematization of my own. As I have already mentioned, I will take *A Grammar of Motives* as the point of departure for my study. As is well known, Burke opened *A Grammar of Motives* by asking, "What is involved, when we say what people are doing and why they are doing it?" (xvii). By beginning with this question and then systematically offering a response to it, Burke provided the grounds for critics to assess the *Grammar* as a book exclusively concerned with the practical art of reading texts. Indeed critics are quite correct when they note that the book does not only declare itself as such but also conforms in its overall structure to a conventional theory-application agenda: part one details the protocols of dramatistic analysis (the pentad); part two applies the set of procedures to seven schools of philosophy; and part three applies the set of procedures to "constitutional" discourses. There can be no doubt that one of the tasks in the *Grammar* is to provide a systematic method for identifying the complex of motives out of which "the various classes of motivational theory" (xxv) were produced. Nonetheless, I will argue in the second chapter that something other than that is also occurring there. In addition to presenting and applying a calculus for determining the motivational center of texts that have been written by others, Burke works over the course of the *Grammar* toward answering the underside of his inaugurating question, What is motive? Put somewhat differently, I will argue that inscribed in the *Grammar* is an attempt to specify the conditions of possibility for human action and individual agency. In this sense I will argue that Burke's *Grammar* is more than an epistemological or critical enterprise and more than a set of directives for extracting the motivational loci out of symbolic forms; it is also a text that seeks, but ultimately fails, to articulate an ontologically guaranteed theory of the subject whose actions cannot be reduced to the playing out of a structure.

In chapter three I will argue that it is possible to read *A Rhetoric of Motives* as a text that reopens the inquiry into motive by seeking to explain not the condition of possibility for individual human action per se but, rather, the condition of possibility for collective human action. That is to say, whereas in chapter two I will argue that *A Grammar of Motives* proffers a theory of the semiautonomous subject, in chapter three I will argue that it is reasonable to read in *A Rhetoric of Motives* a theory of collective subjectivity or identity that cannot be derived merely by generalizing from the individual.

Chapter four will make the claim that *The Rhetoric of Religion: Studies in Logology* is a text that supplements both *A Grammar of Motives* and *A Rhetoric of Motives.* I will argue that this book that stands in the place of the *Symbolic* once again reopens the question of motive not only to specify the condition of possibility for individual and collective action, but also to specify differently the precise nature of their relation. To claim that *The Rhetoric of Religion* supplements the *Grammar* and the *Rhetoric* is not to say that *The Rhetoric of Religion* is only an addition, complement, or appendage to its antecedents; it is also at the same time compensatory. It marks a default or void in the anterior structures.[4] Thus on the one hand I will submit that Burke's concentration on "the principle of the negative" as the logically prior ground of language use per se and hence of the material appearance of the individual and the collective marks a significant addition to his general project; on the other hand I will submit that his logological method of interpretation stands in the place of both the dramatistic and socioanagogic methods advocated in *A Grammar of Motives* and *A Rhetoric of Motives.* Its theoretical assumptions as well as its protocols are described as compensatory to, indeed oftentimes are explicitly advocated as a corrective for, the earlier methods of interpretation.

In the last chapter of the book my point will not be, as I indicated above, merely to dismantle Burke's enterprise. To the contrary, my intent will be to reinvigorate it by specifying the contributions such a reading of Burke's trivium of motives can make to the contemporary discussion about the unique challenges postmodernity poses to social theorists and critics. In order to do so, I will situate Burkeian dramatism and logology in specific relation to Jürgen Habermas's universal pragmatics not simply because Habermas has managed to seize the attention of leading rhetorical theorists and critics, but more importantly because his work represents one of the most serious and sustained engagements with the role of communicative or symbolic action in the formation and reformation of collective life in the late twentieth century. Without discounting the significant contribution Habermas has made toward the development of a postmetaphysical theory of subject and structure, I will argue that a rather radicalized rereading of Burkeian dramatism and logology opens the way toward a theory of the social that, like universal pragmatics, finds in discursive practices the possibility for the articulation of an ontologically secured but nonessentialist theory of social change that does not, however, entail a universalism that disavows differences that matter or insist upon the necessity of a counterfactual realm of self-transparency and idealized discourse. Inscribed within Burke's "principle of the negative," I will argue, are the resources for a resolutely rhetorical theory of social change and human agency that, to modify Stuart Hall's phrase ever so slightly, allows us to discern the ways in which we may transform ourselves in the mirror of politics and, thus, become its new subjects.

2

Reading Ontology in
A Grammar of Motives

There can be no doubt that Kenneth Burke's *A Grammar of Motives* is a book concerned with the practical art of interpreting symbolic acts. Indeed, the introduction and part one of the *Grammar* could have been subtitled "The Protocols of Dramatistic Analysis." First comes a declaration of the project: the book, Burke states, will explain "[w]hat is involved, when we say what people are doing and why they are doing it" (xvii). Second, a massive analytic machinery is posited: the pentad of terms and their ratios that, as a methodological instrument, makes it possible for critics to explicate and assess the motivational loci of discourses by "inquir[ing] into the purely internal relationships which the five terms bear to one another, considering their possibilities of transformation, their range of permutations and combinations" (xviii). Third, the method is given a name, "dramatism," and, finally, a casuistry is chosen, the discourses that constitute the history of Western philosophy. However, in addition to presenting a methodological tool by means of which critics can uncover the motivational loci of symbolic forms, the *Grammar* is also a book that records its author's attempt to come to terms with precisely that which Burke's critical method precomprehends: motive understood in a more originary sense than its particular determinations—as the essence of being human. Hence, I will argue that within the *Grammar* two complicitous but not identical projects are inscribed: one that seeks to offer a means for explaining those processes by which human beings make sense out of their world (method, epistemology) and another that seeks to decipher the nature of the human being that, among other things, produces explanations (ontology). In fact, I will claim that it is by deciphering the *Grammar* as a text moving in these two directions at once that the double function of the pentad is made visible.

On the one hand, the pentad serves as a systematic method for interpreting texts. Burke writes, "any complete statement about motives will offer *some kind of* answers to these five questions: what was done (act), when or where it was done (scene), who did it (agent), how he did it (agency), and why (purpose)" (xvii). On the other hand, the pentad functions as a morphological grid upon which discourses can be grafted to reveal by proxy an internal necessity that inaugurates the production of human action and, thus, human being as such. As Burke puts it, any symbolic action can be "view[ed] . . . ontologically, or in terms of *being,*" insofar as it is looked at "in terms of permanent principles that underlie the process of becoming" (73). In short, I will argue that the *Grammar* is not a book exclusively animated by the desire to present a critical tool that gives us a new take on the ways in which human beings explain their worlds and their place in them. In addition, it is a painstaking and ultimately frustrated investigation of the ontological foundation of motives per se: that which effaces itself in the midst of its appearance.

Revisiting Action and Motion

To have read Burke's work is to be familiar with the action/motion distinction. Indeed, upon asking any reader of Burke's corpus about this pivotal distinction, one invariably receives the same response: "human beings act; things move." It seems as though nothing could be more simple and no other aspect of Burke's thought could be more consistent with mainstream androcentric Western philosophical thought that characteristically divides the world into the human and the nonhuman on the basis of a categorical distinction between that which is active and that which is passive, between being that is a priori capable of transcendence and being that is always already given over to immanence. That Burke perpetuates a philosophical tradition that takes the action/motion or vitalism/mechanism distinction as the architechtonic binary on the basis of which it becomes possible to make sense out of the world and to determine the human being's distinct relation to or place within it finds confirmation in the various speculations on "action" and "motion" scattered throughout part one of the *Grammar*. "Action," according to Burke, is constitutive of human being: it is the primary mode of being human and is to be understood in relation to its dialectical opposite "motion," a term that signifies "sheer locomotion" (85). In support of this distinction, Burke provides the following example: "If one happened to stumble over an obstruction, that would be not an act, but a mere motion. However, one could convert even this sheer accident into something of an act if, in the course of falling, one suddenly *willed* his fall (as a rebuke, for instance, to the negligence of the person who had left the obstruction in the way)" (14). Clearly, motion designates for Burke an act whose character derives solely from "the interaction of forces" (14) over which the agent has no control, those " 'instincts,' 'drives,' or other sheerly compulsive properties" (79) to which the agent necessarily adheres. Burke captures this sense of motion in a later section in the *Grammar* when, in the midst of deriding Hobbes for carrying his theories of mechanism into the moral realm, he invokes the concept-metaphor of the "billiard ball." The movement of the billiard ball proper is an effect solely of physical properties and forces. Indeed, its directionality is determined, in the strictest sense of the word, by a combination of physical, which is to say utterly impersonal, pressures. Put differently, as a motivational ingredient, motion can be likened to "a stimulus" that inaugurates "a response" whose nature is determined "by the sheer disposition of material factors" (10). Similarly, when applied to the realm of human being, the term "motion" names for Burke the moment wherein the subject performs structure.

While "motion is an impersonal principle" (which is to say, neither specific to nor under the control of a particular agent), "action is a personal principle" (76–77), "an arbitrary and magical element . . . undetermined by anything external to the agent" (65). For Burke, the word "action" carries within it "connotations of consciousness or purpose" (14) and marks "a 'doing' rather than being 'done to' " (15). Action, Burke tells us, is "a causa sui" (66): as "an ingredient of every human act," it marks "some measure of motivation that cannot be explained simply in terms of the past, being to an extent, however tiny, a *new thing*" (65). As Wayne Booth puts it, "What [Burke] means by action is that kind of behavior peculiar to a choosing agent, what nonagents like stones and plants and animals cannot perform" (112).[1]

As I noted above, it is generally believed that this distinction between action and motion, between things that move and persons who act, structurally and axiologically determines Burke's approach to human motivation.[2] Indeed, most critics argue that the action/motion binary is the pivotal conceptual distinction out of which Burke later develops an ontology whose contribution lies in the possibility of differentiating the human from the nonhuman.[3] As does Booth, other critics by and large interpret Burke's action/motion dichotomy as the "logical first" by which he is able, in 1968, to differentiate man from all other forms of being. The latter are understood as that class of things that operate exclusively within the realm of necessity or sheer bodily compulsion; the former is understood as that class of beings that necessarily transcend the realm of necessity and dwell in a realm of relative freedom.[4]

I am, of course, far from disputing that this is the case. Just as it is true that Burke resurrects this notion in his later and much celebrated 1968 essay, so too the reading of the action/motion distinction prevalent among critics is quite correct from the existential purview: human beings act, things move. This is not where my point of contestation lies. Rather, in reading this distinction between action and motion as only proposing a differential relationship between the human and the nonhuman, critics theoretically elide what is, perhaps, one of the most productive moments in Burke's work: the tacit suggestion that the difference that obtains *between* the human and the nonhuman, and that indeed structures their relation, also obtains *within* the human being itself.[5]

One can begin to substantiate the claim that for Burke the human being is constituted in and by a resident rift or internal action/ motion differential by turning to a much celebrated (though for different reasons) passage in part one of the *Grammar*. There Burke writes, "[T]he basic unit of action is the human body in purposive motion. We have here a kind of 'lowest common denominator' of action, a minimal requirement that should appear in every act, however many more and greater are the attributes of a complex act. This is the nearest approach which dramatism affords to the 'building block' kind of reduction in materialistic philosophies" (61). If we look closely at this passage we can begin to see that for Burke human acts as such are *nonsimples*. That is to say, human actions are not pure in the sense that their identity is an effect of the absolute displacement or overcoming of motion.[6] To the contrary, human acts are composites whose congealed form is the outcome of the finessing of or subtle negotiation with both an irreducible action or "purpose" component and an irreducible motion component.[7] As Burke puts it on more than one occasion, human actions are "more than motion"; they are "a merger of active and passive" (40) and, thus, register the variable play of these two irreducible motivational loci that reside in the human being.[8] To claim that the action locus of motives and motion locus of motives are both irreducible is of vital significance: if neither action nor motion can be understood as ultimately dominated, absorbed, or subsumed by the other in the moment of the act, then it is neither possible to conceptualize their relation as dialectical in the Hegelian sense of the term (i.e., as a movement toward the supersession of binary terms or substances) nor reasonable to understand the human being's relation to the play of those motivational loci as one of mastery. In fact, it is precisely because the relation of action and motion is one of pure difference that cannot be annulled by a controlling or willing subject that I use the term *finesse* to describe the way in which the human being provisionally and persistently wrestles with a resident antagonism that at once governs and opens the way toward human being that, by virtue of this fecund affiliation, is always already in a state of becoming.

It may appear that when I decipher Burke's statement "the basic unit of action is the human body in purposive motion" as pointing to a requisite discontinuity in the human being, I am taking Burke beyond Burke. This is decidedly not the case. I am merely trying at this point to foreground and underscore those moments in the text that have been passed over by other critics. For instance, little has been made of the fact that Burke rarely speaks of "pure motive." Indeed, on several occasions in part one he warns against doing so. In his section "The Paradox of Purity" Burke writes, "And the ambiguities of substance here take a form that we would call the 'paradox of purity,' or 'paradox of the absolute.' We confront this paradox when deriving the nature of the human person from God as 'super-person,' as 'pure,' or 'absolute' person, since God as a super-person would be impersonal—and the impersonal would be synonymous with the *negation* of personality. Hence, Pure Personality would be the same as No Personality" (35). Following through the logic of the paradox of purity, Burke shows that "pure act" would be the same as "no act" and "pure motive" the same as "no motive." Indeed, it is precisely because the human being's motivational center neither is nor can be reconciled into an identity that "motive" never appears as such. Motive is accessible to us only in its particular determinations: as the "monetary motive," the "symbolic motive," the "rhetorical motive," the "capitalist motive." Again, motive proper is for Burke a principle of structuration rather than a positive presence; an irreconcilable relation between the passive and the active in the human being that is the condition of possibility for being human.[9] I belabor this point because its importance cannot be overemphasized: if we think upon the fact that for Burke motive is the name for the structural differential out of which the human being produces itself, then it becomes possible for us to discern the importance of Burke's use of the term *"homo dialecticus"* (235) as a primary descriptor of the human being. The human being is not, as most readers of Burke would have it, first and foremost a "symbol-using animal." The human being is, rather, first and foremost a dialectical animal,[10] because *dialectic* is a term that I believe signifies for Burke the *process* of the production of the human being, a *movement* that effects verbal or symbolic action but is not limited to these particular determinations.[11]

What all of this suggests is that for Burke the double genesis of motives that makes its appearance in human acts belongs not to the acts proper but, rather, to the subject that produces them. That is to say, whereas the action/motion differential makes its appearance in symbolic action, as a structure it resides in the human being. It is precisely this relation between action and motion, itself structured in and by an irreducible distance, that constitutes the economy of the subject. Read in this way, motive is the name for the structural differential that is the condition of possibility for the historical emergence of the human being in a world.

One need not depend exclusively on the few citations noted above to argue this case. Several sections throughout part one of the *Grammar* seek to draw out and establish the "truth" of this proposition. For example, in a section entitled "Complexity of a Simple Motive" Burke explicitly confronts the tendency on the part of some philosophers and scientists to impute to an act a single motivating ground. He writes, "In keeping with our distrust of both 'perfectionist' and 'invertedly perfectionist' motivations, we should feel justified in *never* taking at its face value any motivational reduction to a 'simple.' As soon as we encounter, verbally or thematically, a motivational simplicity, we must assume as a matter of course that it contains a diversity" (101). It is crucial to notice that Burke does not counter a behaviorist metaphysics by arguing on behalf of the thoroughly autonomous or sovereign subject (pure action). That is to say, he does not substitute one reductive take on human being with another. Instead, he presses the suggestion that all human action, from the most simple to the most complex, cannot be understood as merely the surface manifestation of the play of a single motivational locus, be it motion or action. Indeed, he proceeds to argue that the very appearance or manifest form of the human act is not an outcome of the successful prohibition, displacement, or thorough overcoming of "those 'instincts,' 'drives,' or other sheerly compulsive properties" but, rather, is an effect of an always already precarious and ever-shifting relationship between the two motivational loci that can never be reduced to a one. Burke extends, indeed complicates, this argument in a section of the book that I have already referred to. In the section entitled "The Paradox of Purity" Burke writes, "What we are suggesting here is that . . . all [human acts] embody a *grammatical form* in accordance with which we should not expect a dualism of motives to be automatically dissolved" (38). Having conceived human actions as events produced out of the action/motion differential that resides within the human being, Burke follows the trajectory of his own thought and asserts that the dualism necessarily sustains itself in the materiality of the act. Human acts do not record the sublation of difference into a seamless and self-identical totality. Instead, they register an asymmetrical finessing, record an affiliation (or "partial transformations," in Burke's words [19]), that by virtue of its very provisionality is always already susceptible to change, alteration, reconfiguration. Motive proper, then, is that which lies somewhere between action and motion, mind and body.

What has been the point of this incursion into the "double genesis of motive"? Most certainly, if we take Burke's argument seriously, the action/motion differential Burke presupposes, and to an extent develops, cannot be taken merely as a convenient taxonomy by means of which we can identify the various beings in the world as belonging to the human or nonhuman domains. Moreover, the incursion into the "double genesis of motive" enables us to decipher the double function of the pentad, which, to this point, has been taken merely as a means for interpreting texts.

If, as I have suggested, motive proper is a structure of difference and not a positive presence (it "produces something out of nothing" [66]), and if dialectic is Burke's term for the provisional finessing of that irreducible differential (the outcome of which is a human act), then motive is precisely that which effaces itself in the midst of its material appearance. That is to say, motive proper can never appear as such. The questions then become, How can ontology be anything other than a constantly thwarted attempt to explain the nature of the human being? and Does ontology itself not become little more than a cathected desire to produce an exposition on man?[12]

Something like an opening to these questions is figured in the early pages of the *Grammar* whose patent task is to introduce the five key terms of dramatism. Burke writes, "The titular word for our own method is 'dramatism,' since it invites one to consider the matter of motives in a perspective that, being developed from the analysis of drama, treats language and thought primarily as modes of action" (xxiv). In the pentad Burke had found a model that would enable him to "perceive the generating principle" of all human action by focusing upon particular verbal acts: by "think[ing] of the Grammatical resources as *principles*"—act, scene, agent, agency, and purpose— and in "apply[ing] these principles to temporal situations" (xviii), Burke claims that he will be able to lay bare "the logical substance that is [any particular act's] causal ancestor" (xxi). That is to say, precisely because motive is the differential structure that cannot appear as such, Burke constructs a morphology of human action (the pentad) through which he can grammatically analyze a multiplicity of human acts as "demonstrations" or "illustrations" of the general structure of human activity and, thus, of human being. Conceived as dialectical manifestations or particular determinations of the "permanent principles that underlie the process of becoming" (73), the analysis of human acts in the *Grammar* serves as an inquiry, albeit at one remove, into the subject proper or, as he puts it, into the "motives and relations generic to all mankind ... as a class" (104). Of course, Burke's tactic of taking language and thought as the object of inquiry, when what he really wants to come to terms with is human motivation prior to its particular determinations, finds its logical justification in the paradox of substance. On the paradox of substance he writes:

[T]he word "substance," used to designate what a thing *is,* derives from a word designating something that a thing *is not.* That is, though used to designate something *within* the thing, *intrinsic* to it, the word etymologically refers to something *outside* the thing, *extrinsic* to it. Or otherwise put: the word in its etymological origins would refer to an attribute of the thing's *context,* since that which supports or underlies a thing would be a part of the thing's context. And a thing's context, being outside or beyond the thing, would be something that the thing is *not.* (23)

Despite the fact that, properly speaking, the motive is not the act and the act is not the motive, one can gain access to motive by way of a systematic analysis of the act for which motive has served as the context or generating ground.

For the expressed purpose of reading the *Grammar* as an investigation of the ontological foundation of motive per se, I have narrowly defined the motion differential as a constituent element of a motivational structure located within the human being proper. However, at this juncture I wish to emphasize an aspect of the motion differential only briefly mentioned earlier, namely that Burke's concept of motion as it applies to the human being signifies all those things, biological or otherwise, that constrain or place limits on the free play of the action differential. Hence, subsumed under the motion differential are "instincts," "drives," and "natural forces." Also subsumed under the motion differential (and this is the critical point) is the context within which the human being operates: "the nature of the world as all men necessarily experience it" (xvii).

It is as crucial to notice that for Burke context designates a generalizable ground, and not a specific historical situation, as it is to notice that he indeed accommodates context into his scheme. This is not, of course, an arbitrary move on his part: the nature of his project demands it. He explains at some length:

In our original plans for this project, we had no notion of writing a "Grammar" at all. We began with a theory of comedy, applied to a treatise on human relations. Feeling that competitive ambition is a drastically over-developed motive in the modern world, we thought this motive might be transcended if men devoted themselves not so much to "excoriating" it as to "appreciating" it. Accordingly, we began taking notes on the foibles and antics of what we tended to think of as "the Human Barnyard."

We sought to formulate the basic stratagems which people employ, in endless variations, and consciously or unconsciously, for the outwitting or cajoling of one another. Since all these devices had a "you and me" quality about them, being "addressed" to some person or to some advantage, we classed them broadly under the heading of a Rhetoric. There were other notes, concerned with modes of expression and appeal in the fine arts, and with purely psychological or psychoanalytic matters. These we classed under the heading of Symbolic.

We had made still further observations, which we at first strove uneasily to class under one or the other of these two heads, but which we were eventually able to distinguish as the makings of a Grammar. For we found in the course of writing that our project needed a grounding in formal considerations logically prior to both the rhetorical and the psychological. And as we proceeded with this introductory groundwork, it kept extending its claims until it had spun itself from an intended few hundred words into nearly 200,000, of which the present book is revision and abridgement. (xix–xx)

Given that "[e]ven before we know what act is to be discussed, we can say with confidence that a rounded discussion of its motives must contain a reference to *some kind* of background" (xix), it is imperative that Burke redefine scene as a grammatical category. Mobilizing Ibsen's *An Enemy of the People* in order to substantiate the grammaticalization of context, he explicates the scene-act ratio:

From the motivational point of view, there is implicit in the quality of a scene [context] the quality of the action that is to take place within it. This would be another way of saying that the act will be consistent with the scene. Thus, when the curtain rises to disclose a given stage-set, this stage-set contains, simultaneously, implicitly, all that the narrative is to draw out as a sequence, explicitly. Or, if you will, the stage-set contains the action *ambiguously* (as regards the norms of action)—and in the course of the play's development this ambiguity is converted into a corresponding *articulacy*. The proportion would be: scene is to act as implicit is to explicit. One could not deduce the details of the action from the details of the setting, but one could deduce the quality of the action from the quality of the setting. (6–7)

Taking as his task the specification of the absolute or logically anterior ground of human acts per se, Burke is obliged to bracket out the historically contingent or culturally specific, a prohibition that eclipses "detail" in order to foreground an act's fundamental "quality." In counterdistinction to a Rhetoric and a Symbolic, "a statement about the grammatical principles of motivation" seeks to "lay claim to a universal validity" (xix) and, thus, demands that differences be read as surface and, indeed, inessential variations of an underlying structure.

The point of this somewhat lengthy digression has been to illustrate the way in which the "paradox of substance" serves as the methodological trick by means of which Burke is able to rewrite an implicitly ontological inquiry as an epistemological one. Not only does the paradox of substance enable Burke to focus simply on the text or act since scene (that which is, properly speaking, outside the act) is incorporated within it, but it also enables him to inquire into "the ultimate ground of motives" by grammatically analyzing specifically verbal acts since what is represented or represents itself in symbolic action is a negotiation within an always and already divided agent. As Burke puts it, "the knowledge derived from the act is a knowledge of the act's context, or motivational ground" (41).

Reading Ontology by Proxy

If I am at all correct in my reading of part one of the *Grammar* it becomes possible to actively read parts two and three of the book in a new way. That is to say, we are no longer constrained to read these later sections as others have tended to read them, as only demonstrations or confirmations of the efficacy of the dramatistic method; it also becomes possible to read them as inquiries into motive per se, as attempts on Burke's part to broach the ontophenomenological question "what is motive" by working on actual verbal acts. What I am suggesting in contrast to the interpretations of other critics of the *Grammar* is that parts two and three are more than lessons in how to read[13]; they are also systematic attempts to make legible the logically prior structure of motive, the essence of human being.

I indicated above that the introduction to the *Grammar* could have been subtitled "The Protocols of Dramatistic Analysis." I noted that a declaration of intent is made in it, a massive analytic machinery is posited, and a casuistry is chosen: the discourses that constitute the history of Western philosophy. Burke opens the second part of his book by fulfilling the introduction's declared intent: in one swift and summarizing gesture, he transforms the entire history of Western philosophy into a single, coherent, morphological moment by way of his pentad of terms:

For the featuring of *scene*, the corresponding philosophic terminology is *materialism*.

For the featuring of *agent*, the corresponding terminology is *idealism*.

For the featuring of *agency*, the corresponding terminology is *pragmatism*.

For the featuring of *purpose*, the corresponding terminology is *mysticism*.

For the featuring of *act*, the corresponding terminology is *realism*. (128)

"[S]urveying the entire field at a glance" (128), a plethora of differing philosophical discourses are read as the repetition, substitution, transformation, and permutation of a generating principle. Sequence is rewritten as configuration and an entire span of history is telescoped into a single moment.

At this juncture Burke stops theorizing and begins reading philosophy. For nearly two hundred pages he assumes the perspective of the disinterested morphologist, deciphering "the various schools as languages," using the pentad "as a generating principle that should enable us to 'anticipate' these different idioms" (127). In this way Burke reads Hobbes, Spinoza, and Darwin; Berkeley, Hume, and Leibniz; Kant, Hegel, Marx, and Santayana; Aristotle and Aquinas, appropriately situating each philosopher's discourse on his terminological grid. However, it is in the process of reading Marx that Burke unwittingly exceeds the protocols of his own method and in so doing brings his morphology and, by implication, his theorization of the human being to crisis.

Before marking the break, however, it is necessary to trace out the structure that shapes Burke's grammatical way of reading Marx. Burke begins by offering a traditional reading of Marx that he will later on explicitly undermine. Initially he sees in the various texts the dramatization of a "reversal" of Hegelian idealism. In Marx, Burke notes, the "character of human consciousness in different historical periods [is said to be derived] from the character of the material conditions prevailing at the time" (200). In relation to Hegelian idealism, Marxism can be transposed as "a simple shift from agent to scene as point of origin" (200). This reading fits nicely within Burke's morphology since, as we already know, for the featuring of scene, the corresponding terminology is materialism.

Having said this much, Burke deliberately proceeds to expose the limitations of this reading. He does so by reminding us that Marxists are not simply materialists; they are dialectical materialists. Hence, by way of a simple terminological substitution Burke rewrites dialectical materialists as "idealistic materialist[s]" (200). Granting that "the typical idealistic genealogy is slighted" by the various Marxisms, Burke nevertheless argues that "the idea" or "the agent" is not wholly negated by them. The idea or the agent reappears in the form of social action: "[t]he metaphysical problem of knowledge retreats into the background, [only] to be replaced by the social problem of action" (201). In this doubling gesture, wherein the social is interpreted as signifying both the agent and the scene, Burke identifies "the Marxist modifications of idealism" (201). Operating "with good grammar" Burke resituates Marxism morphologically under the sign of the agent whose corresponding terminology is idealism.

I should note that up to this point Burke's reading of Marxism is grounded on no particular text but on an indeterminate stream of textuality. Perhaps attempting to secure his unconventional reading of Marxism in a concrete way, Burke goes on to produce a close reading of *The Communist Manifesto*. Careful reader that he is, Burke does not fail to note "about fifteen references to the role played by 'conditions' in the motivating of social change" (206). Nonetheless, by way of his grammar Burke sees in this text the rather succinct dramatization of the modification of Hegelian idealism. For Burke, Marx's argument in that text boils down to the call for (purpose) the carrying out of the desired improvements (act) within the logic of a dialectical progression (agency) that can only be realized through the efforts of intending *agents* in the midst of class antagonism (scene). Burke closes his discussion of Marx and Marxism with the following essentialization of his own reading of *The Communist Manifesto:* "precisely where Marxism is most often damned as *materialistic,* is precisely where it is most characteristically idealistic" (214). Having reexpressed Marxism in grammatical terms Burke feels confident that his system has enabled him to produce a more accurate interpretation.

In the midst of all of this, however, something resolutely other has also occurred: that is, the intervention of rhetoric onto the scene of what was supposed to have been purely grammatical reading and rewriting. This is to say, while I am not challenging Burke's interpretation of Marxism, I take issue with his conviction that this operation has been thoroughly grammatical. Despite his own declared intent (to produce "a statement about the grammatical principles of motivation [which] might lay claim to a universal validity" [xix]) and the strict set of procedures he had elaborated ("to inquire into the purely internal relationships which the five terms bear to one another, considering their possibilities of transformation, their range of permutations and combinations—and then to see how these various resources figure in actual statements about human motives" [xviii]), Burke's grammatical reading of *The Communist Manifesto* and ultimate rewriting of Marxist doctrine are two critical gestures that, as I will show, indicate the limits of his morphology and bring his larger project to crisis.

Let us first reconsider Burke's "grammatical" reading of *The Com-*

munist Manifesto, a reading I find shaped by a clandestine respect for Marx's rhetorical inventiveness and, thus, punctuated by rhetorical gestures of its own. To begin, it is no small thing that Burke has selected for his grammatical analysis what has been called Marx's most rhetorical piece of discourse. In vibrant contrast to the philosophical tone of the *Economic and Philosophic Manuscripts,* the scientistic tone of *The Eighteenth Brumaire of Louis Bonaparte,* and the analytical tone of *Capital I, II and III,* the tone of *The Communist Manifesto* is highly dramatic. It is written in a lyrical prose and, indeed, has often been described as a great revolutionary hymn. I am not suggesting that Burke was at all unaware of the rhetorical weight of this document; in fact, if the protocols of his own text did not prohibit it, we might be tempted to interpret the very selection of the text as a rhetorical move on Burke's part, the intended effect of which would be something like the positioning of an ultimate context of justification for his method. Be that as it may, Burke's discussion does open with an explicit commentary on figuration in the *Manifesto.* He says, "The Marxist revision of this dialectic unction opens, with admonitory clangor, in a burlesque of *spirit,* presenting Communism as a *spectre* haunting Europe. (Looking at it thus, I think we can see here something a bit more pointed than a not very fanciful figure of speech. The materialist doctrine that is to be the vessel antithetic to dialectical idealism enters with a mockery of idealism)" (204). This is not an isolated incident. Several times throughout the essay Burke's gaze is diverted from the grammatical relations ruling the text and toward the rhetorical conduct of the text. In one instance Burke goes so far as to note the way in which his own vocabulary "lacks the partisan vigor that infuses the Marxist rhetoric, and makes the *Communist Manifesto* a masterpiece of challenge" (211).

Instances can be multiplied as these rhetorical interventions about Marx's rhetoric are not mere blemishes on an otherwise flawless surface. However, we must not only record Burke's awareness of the rhetorical conduct of Marx's text and the rhetorical flourishes of his own that are produced out of that awareness, but must also look carefully at some of his ways of coping with it. One of these might be Burke's strategy of confronting it head on. At one point in the essay Burke asks, "[W]hat are we to make of the fact that the Manifesto itself is an act of propaganda?" (207)—a question that both is and is not rhetorical. Burke's question must be rhetorical since the protocols of his own text exclude the very possibility of our taking up a question having to do with the " 'you and me' quality about [a discourse], being 'addressed' to some person or to some advantage" (xix). Such concerns fall outside the realm of the grammatical, having been at the outset of this project "classed . . . broadly under the heading of a

Rhetoric" (xix). Thus to the question "what are we to make of the fact that the Manifesto itself is an act of propaganda" we must respond, absolutely nothing at all since rhetoric is not one of our concerns here. At the same time, however, the conduct of Burke's text tells us that the question cannot be taken entirely as a rhetorical gesture: the rest of his essay is a serious response to it.

What are we to make of this precarious moment in Burke's text, this question that both asks about and marks the impossibility of answering to the constitutive role of rhetoric in the construction of discourses? At this juncture we might want to turn to Burke's explicit rewriting of Marxist doctrine. In a section entitled "A Dramatist Grammar for Marxism" (a section, by the way, literally infused by commentary on the rhetoric of Marxism), Burke sets out to provide its "tentative restatement." He describes the enterprise in this way: "We are following no particular text, but are trying to restate the Marxist position in general, as it appears when translated into the terms of characterization employed in this book" (210). Here I will cite only a few lines of this two-page, single-spaced translation: "From the standpoint of society as a whole, an idea is 'active' insofar as it is 'adequate' (that is, insofar as it does accurately name the benign and malign properties of that society). The society must suffer social 'passions' insofar as its ideas are 'inadequate' " (211). It is important to note that any reading of this rewriting is confounded from the start by the impossibility of checking the translation against the original since, as Burke puts it, no "particular text" is invoked. However, I think we can say with some assurance that the grammatical essentialization of Marxism results in a rewriting of material cause (scene) as efficient cause (agent or idea). Accordingly, Burke systematically substitutes one set of terms (words for scene, material conditions, etc.) with another (words for agent or idea).

What we cannot help but notice about Burke's translation is the way in which the grammatically sanctioned and systematic substitution of one terminology for another has substantively altered the "original." While he retains the grammar of Marxism, he produces an articulation that is not Marxist. Thus Burke's grammatically correct translation of Marxist doctrine exposes the very limits of Burke's method by marking the curious moment wherein the "idiom" is inhabited by the idiomatic. That is to say, rather than serving as one more example of the universal applicability of the pentad, Marxism unwittingly performs the inevitable failure of a translation that privileges grammar at the expense of rhetoric. Hence, Burke's initial intent to write rhetoric out puts us on the track of the way in which rhetoric intervenes within the very space opened up by grammar. In fact, when read as the metaphor for the expression that cannot be translated literally precisely because it neither conforms to nor can be explained by the rules of grammar alone, Marxism scandalizes Burke's entire project by refusing to tolerate the grammar/rhetoric distinction upon which Burke had founded his project:

> In our original plans for this project, we had no notion of writing a "Grammar" at all. . . .
>
> We sought to formulate the basic stratagems which people employ, in endless variations, and consciously or unconsciously, for the outwitting or cajoling of one another. . . . we classed them broadly under the heading of a Rhetoric. There were other notes . . . These we classed under the heading of Symbolic.
>
> We had made still further observations, which we at first strove uneasily to class under one or the other of these two heads, but which we were eventually able to distinguish as the makings of a Grammar. For we found in the course of writing that our project needed a grounding in formal considerations logically prior to both the rhetorical and the psychological. (xix–xx)

What was presumed by Burke to be "logically prior" to rhetoric and therefore separate from it is shown in practice to be consubstantial with it.

One more thing should be noted here. I said that Marxism could be read as a metaphor for the idiomatic since it performs the role of that which cannot be fully understood in strictly grammatical terms. However, taken in its conventional and nonpolemic way, the idiomatic names not only an utterance that exceeds grammatical translation but also "a peculiarity of phraseology approved by the *usage* of a language" (*Oxford English Dictionary*, emphasis added). All of this is to suggest that entailed in the idiomatic expression is the history of its uses. Indeed, it is to the history of its uses that we must appeal when trying to make sense out of the idiomatic. When read in this double sense, the idiomatic, which is to say Marxism, not only scandalizes Burke's method by refusing to tolerate the grammar/rhetoric opposition that Burke had accepted at the start; it also brings the morphology to crisis by disclosing it as a less than purely structural enterprise, an enterprise that must admit history.[14] In short, the conscious attempt on Burke's part to morphologize the history of philosophy by way of grammar has been eclipsed by the operation of that which it had previously excluded: rhetoric and history.

What are the consequences of the intervention of rhetoric and history into the space opened up by grammatical reading and rewriting for Burke's larger project? Most important, the unanticipated intrusion discloses Burke's morphology as normative rather than descriptive and, thus, throws into question the explanatory power of the morphology itself. Indeed, inscribed within the method Burke mobilizes in order to reveal by proxy an internal necessity that inaugurates the production of human being as such is the guarantee of a failure. For what Burke has done is graft an ahistorical method onto what is, by his own definition, a resolutely historical albeit nonessential or non–self-identical subject.[15] Put in a different way, the complication arises not fundamentally out of a misfit between Marx and Marxist doctrine and Burke's morphology but, rather, out of a decisive discontinuity between Burke's ontological presuppositions and his morphology. Indeed, in "grounding" his grammar in "formal considerations logically prior to both the rhetorical and the psychological," Burke unwittingly occludes the possibility of assuring the accuracy of his explanation of the human being if only because he seeks to situate his inquiry at an absolute point of origin, a point outside history, anterior to the historical emergence of the human being.[16]

The point here is not, however, to simply identify a miscalculation on Burke's part. To the contrary, the point is to show how, by way of an uncanny inversion, Burke's *Grammar* enables us to begin to compute the relationship of philosophy and history. Just as the rhetoricity of language enables us to detect the limits of a grammar that declares its own universal applicability and, thus, allows us to critique it as a norm (even as grammar allows us to see rhetoricity), so too history makes possible the critique of philosophy. Indeed, the promise of the critique of grammar and philosophy by way of an "originally" historical/rhetorical subject is the gift of this text and the task Burke takes up in *The Rhetoric of Motives*.

3

A Rhetoric of Motives, or Toward an Ontology of the Social

In the previous chapter I argued that one may read in *A Grammar of Motives* an ontology. More specifically, I argued that motive is Burke's name for the irreducible action/motion differential or rift resident in the human being that is the condition of possibility for its historical emergence in a world. In this chapter I will argue that one may read Burke's *A Rhetoric of Motives* as a book that reopens the inquiry into motive by seeking to explain not the condition of the possibility for human action per se but, rather, the condition of possibility for collective action. In short, I want to suggest that written into the *Rhetoric* is an ontology of the social, an ontology of collective being. The specification of that which constitutes for Burke the zero ground or origin of the social is thus the central task of this chapter.

To read in the *Rhetoric* an ontology of the social is to supplement, in the Derridean sense of the term, contemporary Burkeian scholarship since Burke's discussion of the relation between an act and its scene with his attendant theory of identification that opens the book is typically interpreted as a theoretical frame that identifies the general project as a more or less epistemological one and, indeed, one particularly valuable to sociologists inasmuch as Burke stresses the social components of verbal action.[1] Summarizing Burke's predominant task in the *Rhetoric* Hugh Dalziel Duncan writes, "His question is: Who is using what kind of symbols in what situations for what purposes? In the present volume Burke attempts to analyze the ways in which men use symbols to arouse co-operative attitudes in others who must be appealed to in various kinds of social situations" (257). A bit more recently, critics like Bernard Brock and James Chesebro have argued that the *Rhetoric* is an extension of dramatism ("a method for understanding the social uses of language") and have interpreted Burke's theory of identification as "the 'key term' instrumental to understanding" rhetorical discourses and events (Brock 94, 95). Indeed, Chesebro goes so far as to claim that the *Rhetoric*, like Burke's other early writings, is "grounded predominantly, if not exclusively, in an epistemic function of rhetoric" (180).[2] In having taken rhetoric as his object of investigation and in having defined it as an agency that facilitates relations between discrete individuals or as a tool through which "members of a group promote social cohesion" (522), Burke is understood to have set for himself the more general task of providing an explanation of the type of knowledge derived from the experience of existential division and the strategies mobilized for its compensation.[3] Thus critics tend to decipher the *Rhetoric* as an extensive account of how rhetorical discourse serves as the means through which human beings overcome social estrangement or, at least, attempt to do so. As Christine Oravec states in a recent essay that seeks to explicate what she calls the "transference of association [which] takes place between persons as well as between areas of an individual's own concerns" (183), "[l]anguage then serves as a material mediator between history and the individual" (182).

To read Burke's *Rhetoric* as a book that seeks to explain the means through which human beings attempt to overcome the heterogeneity of the social sphere by producing identifications is not without plausibility. Burke's decision to broaden the scope of his investigation so as to include the relation between an act and the scene within which it takes place can certainly be taken as the sign of a serious attempt to pull out of dramatistic analysis those resources necessary for understanding the quandaries of social life, the complexities of "acting-together." Indeed, in the *Rhetoric* the notion of the autonomous act that animated the *Grammar* opens out to the notion that any act springs up within and contributes to a larger chain of acts that we might just as well call history.[4] As more than one critic has noted, such transformation from the *Grammar* to the *Rhetoric* is most vividly recorded in and by a reconceptualization of "scene." In the latter book Burke brackets the grammaticality of scene and redefines it as a heuristic category confounded by a multiplicity of factors not necessarily recorded in the act per se. As he puts it, "As regards 'autonomous' activities, the principle of Rhetorical identification may be summed up thus: The fact that an activity is capable of reduction to intrinsic, autonomous principles does not argue that it is free from identification with other orders of motivation extrinsic to it. Such other orders are extrinsic to it, as considered from the standpoint of the specialized activity alone. . . . 'Identification' is a word for the autonomous activity's place in this wider context, a place with which the agent may be unconcerned" (551). In contrast to the specification it had received in the *Grammar*, scene here designates a plethora of relations that obtain between a "specialized activity" (and, thus, its corresponding agent) and the social, economic, and political orders out of which it is produced and to which it contributes.

Moreover, Burke does provide a theory that seems to explain explicitly the way in which both overt attempts at persuasion and more subtle means of identification transform the heterogeneity of the social into a relatively homogeneous, albeit hierarchical, sphere. Indeed, in his much celebrated essay in the *Rhetoric* entitled "Positive, Dialectical and Ultimate Terms," which presents what might aptly be called a typology of rhetorics, Burke explicitly tries to account for the way in which discourses promote social cohesion between estranged individuals.

Critics also find ample justification for interpreting Burke's *A Rhetoric of Motives* as an extended exposition on rhetoric as the means through which a collective will is organized, the instrumentality by means of which multiple competing individualities and interests are transformed into what Burke calls a social hierarchy in his thumbnail definition of "identification." He writes, "A is not identical with his colleague, B. But insofar as their interests are joined, A is *identified* with B. Or he may *identify himself* with B even when their interests are not joined, if he assumes that they are, or is persuaded to believe so" (544). Through either explicit attempts at persuasion or more subtle forms of identification, A becomes identified with B: the supersession of the individual and the consolidation of the social are accomplished by rhetorical exchange.

I do not wish to argue against the aforementioned interpretation of Burke's *Rhetoric*, but in addition to recognizing the insights it affords us into the formative role rhetoric plays in the constitution of the socius, I also want to underscore one of its limits: namely, the assumption that rhetoric or language is the sufficient cause of the social for Burke. In counterdistinction to those critics who read the book as a strictly epistemological project, I will argue that a careful reading of part three of the *Rhetoric*, wherein we witness a qualitative shift in Burke's conception of language and rhetoric from means or agency that facilitates social cohesion to his conception of language as *"containing* within it the motive force of sociality" (emphasis added), suggests that for Burke the question "what are the conditions of the possibility for the social?" cannot be answered so simply. Indeed, if taken seriously the qualitative shift in Burke's conception of language and rhetoric is a textual event that signifies more than a mere slipup or unsubstantiated refutation of the "rhetoric as epistemic" position; it also signifies an effort to come to terms with the social as a structural possibility logically anterior to its historical emergence in language and through rhetoric. I think this is what is at stake in the *Rhetoric*, a book whose driving problematic may be stated as follows: rhetoric, and language more generally, are necessary for the historical emergence of social formations, but neither language nor rhetoric can be posited as the sufficient cause of the social.[5] What, then, is the condition of possibility for the social?

Reconstituting Action and Motion

Burke's theoretical allegiance to a conception of rhetoric as the means through which the malaise of competing individualities and interests ("the Region of the Scramble") is symbolically transformed into the symmetry and mystical unity of the social is compromised, or at least made indefinite, by the following declaration that appears in part three of the *Rhetoric*: "[T]o say that man is a symbol-using animal is by the same token to say that he is a 'transcending animal.' Thus, there is in language itself a motive force calling man to transcend the 'state of nature' (that is, the order of motives that would prevail in a world without language, Logos, 'reason')" (716). Here Burke is not, as many critics presume, merely amplifying his discussion on rhetoric as the vehicle that shuttles between human beings and history, human beings and the public sphere. Something else is going on; another theoretical terrain is being opened up. Of that much we can be certain. What is less certain, however, is the precise nature and value of this domain whose proper name is not rhetoric but *language* and whose distinguishing characteristic is its intimate association with a transcending motive. What does Burke mean when he says "there is in language itself a motive force calling man to transcend the 'state of nature' "?

The difficulty in interpreting this statement arises out of Burke's use of the preposition *in*. Is Burke suggesting that the "transcending motive" is indigenous to language per se? Is he positing language as the absolute origin of an economy of motive out of which social forms emerge? Or does the "transcending motive," with the social forms it inaugurates, find its origin elsewhere, in a space exterior to language per se?

One way of closing in on this question is to move to another place in the text where language is named and analyzed in relation to social formations, a section entitled "Pure Persuasion" that appears toward the end of the *Rhetoric*. I will plot the general movement of Burke's argument in this section of the *Rhetoric* since I shall propose that his specification of what is meant by "pure persuasion" serves as a passage toward something like an ontology of the social.

In these twenty-odd pages, Burke seeks not only to expose the limits of both the economistic and psychologistic explanations of the emergence of social formations but also to integrate such explanations into a larger and all-inclusive system grounded on a "hierarchic incentive (with its 'mystery') embedded in the very nature of language" (802). To make his argument, Burke begins with a note against the psychoanalytic interpretation of literary texts. He takes as his own privileged examples Empson's analysis of *Alice in Wonderland* and what is presented as the generally accepted interpretation of *Lady Chatterley's Lover* and *The Book of the Courtier*. Contrary to Empson's and the general but informed opinion, Burke claims that the psychoanalytic interpretation of these books conceals a great deal more than it reveals.[6] By "see[ing] too clearly" the "sexual" thematic, psychoanalytic interpretation fails to specify the true underlying motivational locus that structures these books; it "conceal[s] the rhetorical exercise, the artistic persuasion, emboding [sic] motives not of sexual but of social intercourse" (791–92). Contrary to standard psychoanalytic lore, "Each [book], in its way, is not merely a work that implicitly embodies the principle of courtship: in all three the principle of courtship is explicitly the subject matter" (792). In each of these books Burke identifies as central the thematic of courtship to which corresponds an underlying stratum of motive he calls "hierarchy in general" with its attending effect of "mystery." Having not only located but also recognized as central the "hierarchical incentive," a motive whose precarious success is defined and perpetually sustained by a structure of distance, Burke sets up the conditions for a general inquisition into the rhetorical per se. As he puts it, distance or "standoffishness" is the necessary condition of courtship, and "[t]his purely technical pattern is the precondition of *all* appeal" (795).

Burke does write at some length about this structure of distance or interval that is the precondition of all rhetorical acts, arguing that if a unity between the source of appeal and its designated end were theoretically attainable the rhetorical per se would not be a structural possibility. He says, "For if union is complete, what incentive can there be for appeal? Rhetorically, there can be courtship only insofar as there is division. Hence, only through interference could one court

44 / Addressing Postmodernity

continually, thereby perpetuating genuine 'freedom of rhetoric' " (795). Obviously Burke does not attribute the perpetual rebirth of rhetoric to accidental forces; he defines it as something arising out of a natural necessity. The precise character of this natural necessity is not specified in this passage, although he does tell us that it is "implicit in the 'transcendent' nature of symbolism itself" (795). Here Burke's use of the word *implicit* is key because it signifies a premise indispensable to his explanation of the emergence of social forms: that an underlying stratum of motive is implied or makes its appearance in language. In positing a separation of language (and rhetoric) and an underlying stratum of motive that is its condition of possibility, Burke's own text renders less plausible the proposition that for Burke language is the zero ground of the social. Indeed, the rest of this short section in the *Rhetoric* works against such a proposition by locating the "aptitude" of sociality (what Burke calls "pure persuasion") not in language, though it is most certainly in language that it becomes visible to us, but in the human being per se as "*homo dialecticus.*"

However, what is it about man as *homo dialecticus* that assures the emergence of the social? I argued in the previous chapter that one can read in the *Grammar* something like an ontology of the human being. It was my claim that written into the *Grammar* is the thesis that the historical emergence of the human being per se is predicated in the provisional finessing of an irreducible and resident action/motion differential. In other words, the action/motion differential is the economy of the human being. I bring this up because I want to argue here that this definition of the human being is taken as Burke's point of departure in the *Rhetoric*. Indeed, it is by way of an amplification of this definition of man that Burke formulates an answer to the question, What is it about man as *homo dialecticus* that assures the emergence of the social?

The passage from the "state of nature" to "the Region of the Scramble"[7] finds its metaphysical guarantee in the nature of the human being prior to its emergence into history, prior to its emergence into language.[8] Although, as Burke writes, "[t]he intensities, morbidities, or particularities of mystery [which is to say, the social] come from institutional sources," nonetheless "the *aptitude* comes from the nature of man, generically, as a *symbol-using animal*" (803). Here, as in the *Grammar*, Burke is attentive to the two constituent components whose variable relation but irreducible difference constitutes the human being as such. Once again he insists that human action is rooted in the dynamic interaction of the action locus of motives ("symbol-using") and the motion locus of motives ("animal"). This is not to say, however, that the *Rhetoric* merely reiterates what had been proposed before. To the contrary, though the action/motion differential cannot be read as if it had no history, a new determination is written into the *Rhetoric,* one out of which an ontology of the social figures forth.

I will start with the concept of motion rather than with the concept of action as an ontological determinant since, and this is not a justification in the absolute sense,[9] access to the latter can more easily be had once the calculus of the former has been fixed. As I indicated above, the concept of motion exceeds in the *Rhetoric* its specification in the *Grammar.* It signifies more than "the interaction of forces" over which the human being has no control, more than the " 'instincts,' 'drives,' or other sheerly compulsive properties" to which the human being necessarily adheres, and, indeed, more than "the sheer disposition of material factors" that ascribe to human action an absolute limit. In addition to all of the above, motion is a term that signifies a chronic condition of the human being, its nonidentity with and its estrangement from all other members of the species. Motion is Burke's name for a certain alterity, an alterity that definitively prohibits a perfect conjuncture between man and man.[10] To what does Burke attribute this unbroachable estrangement, this radical disjunction between human beings that constitutes the self as irreducibly other? He attributes it to "the *individual centrality of the nervous system,* in the *divisiveness* of the individual human organism, from birth to death" (654). Human beings are "*biologically* estranged" (639); theirs is a "generic divisiveness which, being common to all men, is a universal fact about them" (670). Thus contrary to Marx and to Freud, Burke claims the human being is always and already estranged. Indeed, this estrangement is "prior to any divisiveness caused by social classes" (670) and/or psychosexual development. The principle of individuation or division "is grounded not socially, but biologically" (669). There is "an individual divisiveness prior to all class cohesion . . . prior to the social" (671) and its origin is to be located in the act of birth: "In parturition begins the centrality of the nervous system" (670). Estrangement is a biological, indeed ontological, fact: it is inscribed in the nature of the human being proper.[11]

It is from within the newly determined calculus of motion that it becomes possible to detect the way in which Burke's specification of action in the *Rhetoric* exceeds its prior specification in the *Grammar:* it signifies more than "some measure of motivation that cannot be explained simply in terms of the past"; it connotes, over and above "consciousness or purpose," "a 'doing' rather than being done to." Indeed, if motion has come to signify the ontologically secured estrangement of man, action is now its dialectical opposite. Just as it is of man's essence to be cut off from all others as an other, so too it is of his essence to seek to "transcend [this] 'state of nature' " (716). Here, then, action signifies the " 'rationality' of *homo dialecticus*," the "[r]esources of classification, of abstraction, of comparison and contrast, of merger and division, of derivation, and the like" that "characterize the thinking of man *generically*" (809). Action is, in other words, Burke's term for the "super-personal" capacities "inborn to man" that make it possible for him to imaginatively identify with an other.

Now a pause is in order, for what Burke has announced here is nothing less than the human being's "generic aptitude" for sociality. Action marks not only the human being's insatiable desire to transcend those " 'instincts,' 'drives,' or other sheerly compulsive properties" directly attributable to the body and to nature, but also its desire to break out of the imprisonment of individuality and merge with the other. Indeed, it is within this prelinguistic, prehistoric locus of motive that all the resources of sociality are to be found.

To this point I have tried to establish that in the *Rhetoric* the two constituent motivational loci that constitute the irreducible differential out of which the human being produces itself are newly determined: motion is redefined as the principle of individuation and action is redefined as the principle of sociality. Taken together, the action and motion loci of motives constitute the zero ground of the social. The "roots of ownership," the roots of "ideology," of "class," of "courtship," of "hierarchy," indeed of "social cohesion" per se

reside in the *individual centrality of the nervous system,* in the *divisiveness* of the individual human organism, from birth to death[.] What the body eats and drinks becomes its special private property; the body's pleasures and pains are exclusively its own pleasures and pains. True, there is vicarious sharing by empathy, by sympathy, the "imaginative" identification with one another's states of mind. And there is the mutuality of cooperation and language whereby human society becomes, not an aggregate of isolated individuals, but a superentity, involving principles of interdependence that have in the past gone by such names as rationality, consciousness, conscience, and "God." (654)

In the *Rhetoric* Burke's thinking of the social finds its resources in the newly determined space of the individual: in the predication of the human being per se is the possibility of the social.[12]

Rereading Identification

If the newly determined structure of the human being is the condition of possibility for the social, what inaugurates its historical emergence? Identification, a "key" concept whose full implications I have bracketed until now, is Burke's name for the ontologically guaranteed but genuinely historical process whereby a condition of impossibility (the irreducible estrangement of the individual) is dialectically transformed or sublated into a condition of possibility (sociality) by way of rhetoric.

To be sure, when Burke addresses identification his preoccupation with questions of origin gives way to a preoccupation with questions of process, his concern with structure gives way to a preoccupation with history. For example, he writes: "Bring together a number of individual nervous systems, each with its own unique centrality, and from this indeterminate mixture of cooperation and division there emerge the conditions for the 'basic rhetorical situation' " (654). Here Burke has abandoned the project of the thinking of Being and has taken up the task of the thinking of beings. It is precisely the co-presence of human beings at a historical conjuncture that sets up the conditions for the material appearance of the social. In other words, it is out of a historical convergence of human beings, each of whom is constituted in and by an irreducible action/motion differential, that the call to identification issues forth.[13]

Identification does not, however, produce a unity in the proper sense of the word.[14] Indeed, this is what Burke seems to want to establish early in the *Rhetoric* as he defends his "titular term" identification. "[T]o begin with 'identification' is," he claims, "by the same token, though roundabout, to confront the implications of *division*" (546). He writes, "In being identified with B, A is 'substantially one' with a person other than himself. Yet at the same time he remains unique, an individual locus of motives. Thus he is both joined and separate, at once a distinct substance and consubstantial with another" (545). In the historical moment of identification, the human being "both is and is not one" with that other. That is to say, the social is always and already both a concurrence and an irreproachable distance, both a fusion and a separation.[15]

In defining the social as a unity that both is and is not, Burke opens up the seeming unity of the social and draws the reader's attention to the fact that the social is a catachresis, a "mystery." It is a thing to which there belongs no proper referent, "a communion of estranged entities" (701).[16] The social, which is to say the "we," is what might be called in contemporary parlance a textual chain, a "reality" woven of discontinuities and constitutive differences.[17]

This insight is crucial, for in having seen in the concrete instance of identification a heterogeneity, Burke is able to bring into focus the economy of the social. It is precisely on the basis of the maintenance of a disjunction between human beings that the social both makes its appearance and is sustained. In a passage to which I have already referred, Burke notes, "This purely technical pattern is the precondition of *all* appeal. And 'standoffishness' is necessary to the form, because without it the appeal could not be maintained. For if union is complete, what incentive can there be for appeal? Rhetorically, there can be courtship only insofar as there is division. Hence, only through interference could one court continually, thereby perpetuating genuine 'freedom of rhetoric' " (795). Burke gives expression to this same notion in his earliest discussion of identification. He writes, "Identification is affirmed with earnestness precisely because there is division. Identification is compensatory to division. If men were not apart from one another, there would be no need for the rhetorician to proclaim their unity. If men were wholly and truly of one substance, absolute communication would be of man's very essence" (546). Although I will return to these significant passages in the final chapter of this book, what is crucial to notice at this juncture is that, paradoxically enough, the economy of the social is an opposition between the human aptitude for sociality and the human aptitude for individuation. The convergence of a plurality of human beings (each animated by this double genesis of motive) at a given historical moment sets into motion the dialectical process of the production of the social. Thus between the possibility for exchange and an unbroachable estrangement, and by way of a dialectical movement, the social appears not as a perfectly egalitarian space of cooperation but always and already as a field necessarily fraught with factional strife.

From Ontology to the Question of Rhetoric

Just as it is important to notice that for Burke identification is an economy that never yields a unity as such and, thus, makes possible the incessant production of social forms, so too it is important to remember that for Burke the social is not a textual chain whose origins and ends are altogether shifting and provisional. As I argued above, Burke attributes the social and all of its logical permutations to the irreducible, differential, and, indeed, productive tension between the action and motion loci of motives resident to *homo dialecticus*. This leaves one in a kind of quandary, however, for if the action/motion differential resident to the human being is the zero ground of the social, and if identification is the dialectical process through which the social historically appears always and already as an imperfect and, thus, provisional sublation, what about language and rhetoric, the subject proper of this book?

To be sure, language and rhetoric cannot be understood as the origin proper of the social if one reads in the *Rhetoric* an ontology that posits a space anterior or logically prior to it, a space out of which the social emerges. However, such reading by no means obliges one to conclude that language and rhetoric are just two epiphenomena among others for Burke. Indeed, Burke writes at great length to convince us that this simply is not the case. For example, in the third part of the *Rhetoric* he explicitly challenges Carlyle's suggestion that a relation of equivalence obtains between word-using and tool-using. Burke writes:

> So, all told, though there are respects in which words and mechanical inventions may be classed together, as instruments ("weapons"), there are also important respects in which they must be distinguished.
> And these considerations allow for a distinction between verbal productive forces (the nature of "rationality" or "human consciousness") and the "forces of production" in the economic sense (tools invented by operations of the human brain and transmitted with the help of vocabulary). (812–13)

The crucial point here, of course, is that a distinction is to be made between language and rhetoric and all other human productions, namely, that word-using with the logic entailed therein is, in fact, the *mode* of production of all other human contrivances (i.e., clothing, money, tools, machines, and indeed institutions themselves). As Burke puts it, "Out of his symbols, man has developed all his inventions" (660).

To read language and rhetoric as the mode of production of the social (in the strictest philosophical sense of the word) is, of course, to work explicitly against those critics who interpret Burke's *Rhetoric* as having posited language and rhetoric as the absolute origin of the social. I have already expressed my disagreement with this account at some length. Here, however, it is necessary for me to underscore the difference between my own reading and the reading offered by other critics who take language and rhetoric not necessarily as the origin of the social (and, thus, avoid making the more radical "rhetoric as epistemic" claim) but, rather, as the means or instrumentality through which the social is constructed. In claiming that the symbolic is the *mode* of production of the social for Burke, I do not intend to suggest that language and rhetoric are merely intermediary agents interposed or intervening between the human being and history. Instead, I am suggesting that the symbolic (and its concomitant logic) is itself the form in which the social, indeed history itself, approaches sense.[18] Put differently, it is in language and rhetoric that the social takes place: language and rhetoric are the way of being of the social; language and rhetoric are the very mode of existence of the social.[19] This is what Burke seems to be suggesting when he writes:

[T]he logic of symbols must be "prior" to the effects of any "productive forces" in the socio-economic meaning of that expression. And one should not forget that the productive forces themselves owe much of their development to linguistic agencies, not merely in the sense that vocabulary is needed for guiding the production of complex instruments and for maintaining the tradition of their use, but also in a more radical sense. For the distinctive insight in human invention is not the use of tools, since animals use tools; it is in the use of tools for making tools. And this insight-at-one-remove, this reflexive pattern, is much like the insight of language itself, which is not merely speech about things (a dog's barking at a prowler could be called that), but speech about speech. This secondary stage, allowing for "thought of thought," is so integrally connected with the human power to invent tools for making tools, that we might call such power linguistic in essence. (701–2)

The social is organized, that is to say, it makes its material appearance in symbolic production. The truth of the matter is that the material appearance of any particular social form is purely and simply linguistic or symbolic production itself operating under determinate conditions. "Thus, one particular order (or property structure), with its brands of 'mystery,' may be better suited than another for the prevailing circumstances" (803). However, and this is the important point, "in any [social] order, there will be the mysteries of hierarchy, since such a principle is grounded in the very nature of language" (803).

I have argued in this chapter that it is possible to read in Burke's *A Rhetoric of Motives* an ontology of the social. I also underscored the fact that such reading supplements contemporary Burkeian scholarship, the dominant trend of which is to interpret this work as an epistemological enterprise. One might think these readings of the book confront one another in hostility, each declaring the other's poverty, the other's blindness. Could it not be the case, however, that the readings do not so much represent a confrontation between one another as mark a duplicity in the book, a duplicity harbored in "the wondrous agency of *Symbols*" whose magic engenders "a doubled significance" (644)? Such a thought is enabling, for from within such a perspective one would not have to choose absolutely between one interpretation or the other; one would not be obliged to privilege epistemology or ontology. One would be required instead to "meditate upon the circularity which makes them pass into one another indefinitely" (Derrida 1982b, 173). And such thought would, as I have tried to suggest, take us to the farthest reaches of the *Rhetoric* and, as I will claim in the next chapter, make it possible for us to move otherwise into *The Rhetoric of Religion: Studies in Logology.*

4

Further Speculations on the Dialectic: *The Rhetoric of Religion*

Although much has been made of what Kenneth Burke has called logology, very little attention has been paid to his inaugural book-length manuscript on the subject entitled *The Rhetoric of Religion: Studies in Logology*. Oddly enough even less attention has been paid to its third chapter wherein Burke applies logological analysis to the creation myth, a story he identifies as "just about *perfect* for the purposes of the 'logologer' " (3). Indeed, in the attempt to come to terms with Burke's "doctrine of the *Logos*" (Burke 1985, 89), critics by and large pay mere homage to the book; for the most part their substantive statements about logology derive from articles Burke published at least a decade after he finished writing the original three hundred–odd pages on the subject.[1]

Contrary to the prevailing tendency on the part of critics to interpret the logological enterprise from within the frame presented in Burke's most recent essays, I will take as my own point of departure the book itself. Indeed, it will be my suggestion here that a critical approach that takes as its first order of business a careful charting of the protocols of *The Rhetoric of Religion* but is willing to follow the precarious rule of textual aporias "which harbors the unbalancing of the equation, the sleight of hand at the limit of a text which cannot be dismissed simply as a contradiction" (Spivak 1976, xlix) makes it possible to produce a supplementary reading of the book that goes beyond not only its declared claims but also the claims in Burke's later essays on logology as well. Specifically, I will argue that such a strategy of reading enables us to detect the way in which Burke, one, reopens the question of the condition of possibility for the historical emergence of individual and collective being; two, exposes his earlier theorization of their emergence in *A Grammar of Motives* and *A Rhetoric of Motives* as inadequate, by way of the principle of the negative; three, imperfectly exploits the critical resources of the principle of the negative; and four, unwittingly discloses the limits of logology itself. Here I should stress that my interest is not to dismantle the dramatistic-logological project. To the contrary, my ultimate aim will be to reinvigorate it by deploying precisely that which has been "repressed" or, as Burke himself would put it, "discounted" by the text—the full force of the negative.

A Reading Lesson

In his 1985 article entitled "Dramatism and Logology," Kenneth Burke takes up the question, "why *two* terms [dramatism and logology] for *one* theory"? In uncharacteristically lucid fashion, he posits the following answer: " 'Dramatism' . . . features what we humans *are* (the symbol-using animal). Logology is rooted in the range and quality of *knowledge* that we acquire when our bodies (physiological organisms in the realm of non-symbolic motion) come to profit by their peculiar aptitude for learning the arbitrary, conventional mediums of communication called 'natural' languages (atop which all sorts of specialized nomenclatures are developed, each with its particular kind of insights)" (89–90). To this and other similar statements Burke has recently published, critics attach a particular privilege: they are repeatedly invoked as the authoritative explanation of the purpose and place that *The Rhetoric of Religion: Studies in Logology* has in Burke's system. Indeed, by means of this declaration, everything is made to fall into place: dramatism is Burke's name for his ontology; logology is the name for his epistemology.

One could, of course, question the assumptions that enable critics to fix the function of *The Rhetoric of Religion* in this way, such as the assumption that hindsight is twenty-twenty or, to put it differently, that the oppositional relation between the subject and the object of retrospection, "upon which the possibility of objective descriptions rests," is uncontaminated "by the patterns of the subject's desire as is the subject constituted by that never-fulfilled desire" (Spivak 1976, lix). However, rather than rehearse in theoretical terms the question of whether Burke (or any writer for that matter) has direct access to his meaning, I should like to take another tack, once again working against the current of contemporary Burkeian scholarship to raise a somewhat different question, namely, why two books on the same subject?

Despite what the history of Burkeian criticism would lead us to believe, Burke has written not one but two rhetorics—*A Rhetoric of Motives* and *The Rhetoric of Religion*. This fact is all the more striking if one abides by Burke's autobiographical comments scattered throughout the prefaces to his earlier books. Not only does *The Rhetoric of Religion* perform a doubling, a folding back onto a thematic that had been determined nearly twenty years before, but it also marks a failure of sorts—the breaking of a promise. *The Rhetoric of Religion* stands in the place of the *Symbolic of Motives*, the projected third and final volume of Burke's trilogy on motives.[2] What then does one do with this book that reiterates a past and defers a future-present?

It would not be far from the truth to say that the deferral of a future-present is the declared secular aim of *The Rhetoric of Religion*. Indeed, its worldly aspiration is to keep that which has appeared on the horizon of human history at a distance. Burke writes:

[T]hough the logologer cannot hope to offer the reader something even remotely approaching either the vast ultimate promises or the equally vast ultimate threats which the theologian holds forth, there is at least an important "moral" to be drawn from this study. It derives from the great stress we have laid upon the sacrificial principle which, we try to show, is intrinsic to the idea of Order. If we are right in what we take the Creation Myth in Genesis to be saying, then the contemporary world must doubly fear the cyclical compulsions of Empire, as two mighty world orders, each homicidally armed to the point of suicide, confront each other. As with dominion always, each is much beset with anxiety. And in keeping with the "curative" role of victimage, each is apparently in acute need of blaming all its many troubles on the other, wanting to feel certain that, if the other and its tendencies were but eliminated, all governmental discord (all the Disorder that goes with Order) would be eliminated. (4)

How does one manage to keep at bay a future that is already written into the present? Although, as Burke cautions, there are no guarantees, one can begin by determining nothing less than the origin of human history and the logic of its development, and this can be accomplished by studying the workings of language and rhetoric, the mode of production of the social: "For however the world is made, that's how language is made" (272).

Here, of course, the suggestion is already being made that *The Rhetoric of Religion* exceeds the limits proper of epistemology if, as Burke puts it in his 1985 article "Dramatism and Logology," we mean by epistemology "the range and quality of *knowledge* that we acquire when our bodies . . . come to profit by their peculiar aptitude for learning the arbitrary, conventional mediums of communication" (89–90). In fact, the trick is to recognize that by way of the circuitous route of language and through the help of an analogic, the origin of social or collective being (what I called human history) and the logic of its development can be deciphered as well. As Burke puts it, "these forms can be further studied not directly as knowledge but as anecdotes that help reveal for us the quandaries of human governance" (268).

If the ultimate aim of logology is to appreciate the origin and logic out of which "the quandaries of human governance" arise by studying theological anecdotes,[3] the specific task of *The Rhetoric of Religion: Studies in Logology* is to teach us how to read them. Indeed, help in reading theological texts comes in the chapter that opens the book proper. "On Words and The Word" both announces a coherent set of theoretical assumptions regarding language and its use and prescribes a corresponding method of analysis.

The chapter comprises six interrelated analogies, all of which are firmly rooted in the observable fact that although " '[w]ords' . . . have wholly naturalistic, empirical reference . . . they may be used analogically, to designate a further dimension, the 'supernatural' " (7). Such an observation is, Burke cautions, deceptively simple: "For whereas the words for the 'supernatural' realm are necessarily borrowed from the realm of our everyday experiences, out of which our familiarity with language arises, once a terminology has been developed for special theological purposes the order can become reversed. We can borrow back the terms from the borrower, again secularizing to varying degrees the originally secular terms that had been given 'supernatural' connotations" (7). Not only does Burke point out that language use, what Saussure would call *parole,* is beset from the start by a paradox—it has "its Upward Way and Downward Way" (8)—he also demonstrates that the language of the everyday, that is, colloquial speech, performs a metalepsis of sorts. For example:

Consider the word "grace," for instance. Originally, in its Latin form, it had such purely secular meanings as: favor, esteem, friendship, partiality, service, obligation, thanks, recompense, purpose. Thus, *gratiis,* or *gratis* meant: "for nothing, without pay, through sheer kindness," etc. The pagan Roman could also say "thank God" (*dis gratia*)—and doubtless such early usage contributed to the term's later availability for specifically theological doctrine. But in any case, once the word was translated from the realm of social relationships into the supernaturally tinged realm of relationships between "God" and man, the etymological conditions were set for a reverse process whereby the *theological* term could in effect be *aestheticized,* as we came to look for "grace" in a literary style, or in the purely secular behavior of a hostess. (7–8)

By way of a kind of forgetting, the symbol-using animal reinstates in the secular realm terms that have been used analogically to talk about the supernatural. In so doing cause is unwittingly substituted for effect and the "natural" is infused with the properties linguistically attributed to the supernatural.

The exchange of properties between the natural and the supernatural that takes place in language use is neither an isolated phenomenon that can be discounted as an exception nor a mere mistake that can be corrected by straightening out the chronology. According to Burke, the transference of properties so elegantly displayed in the relation between secular and profane discourse is, in fact, a structural property of language itself. All language use exhibits this transcending, metaleptical property:

> The quickest and simplest way to realize that words "transcend" non-verbal nature is to think of the notable difference between the kind of operations we might perform with a *tree* and the kind of operations we might perform with the *word* "tree." Verbally, we can make "one tree" into "five thousand trees" by merely revising our text, whereas a wholly different set of procedures would be required to get the corresponding result in nature. Verbally, we can say, "To keep warm, cut down the tree and burn it" and we can say this even if there is no tree. (8–9)

There is, then, "a sense in which the *word* for tree 'transcends' the thing as thoroughly as does the Platonic ideal of the tree's perfect 'archetype' in heaven" (10). In fact, it is precisely by way of this tropological operation that language is able not only to work but also to add "a 'new dimension' to the things of nature (an observation that would be the logological equivalent of the theological statement that grace perfects nature)" (8).

Burke's concentration on this "sheerly *technical* kind of 'transcendence' " (10) that language use necessarily performs leads him to draw out six highly theoretical analogies: "the 'words-Word' analogy; the 'Matter-Spirit' analogy; the 'Negative' analogy; the 'Titular' analogy; the 'Time-Eternity' analogy; and the 'Formal' analogy" (38). At this point I should like to take up the somewhat cumbersome task of explicating each of the analogies since it will be my claim that when taken together they give us an interpretive strategy that is very different from the one presented in *A Grammar of Motives* and *A Rhetoric of Motives*, one that takes the essentialization of the temporal as its general rule.

Burke's first analogy, "that between 'words' (lower case) and 'The Word' (in capitals)" (11), seeks to establish "the likeness between words about words and words about The Word" (33). After moving through a somewhat truncated philological investigation that establishes good reason for "resisting a tendency to equate 'Logos' [The Word (of) God] too strictly with 'Reason' " (12) and through a brief analysis of the relation between "the first and second persons of the Trinity" as formally equivalent to the relation between "the *thought* that leads to utterance [and] the *uttered word* that expresses the thought," Burke posits the first analogy, "from which all the other analogies could be deduced" (13): "What we say about *words,* in the empirical realm, will bear a notable likeness to what is said about *God,* in theology" (13–14). Thus, midway into the first analogy, Burke establishes the "architectonic" principle from which the other conventions and operations of logological interpretation follow. As R. E. Garlitz explains in an article that seeks to explicate the developmental relation between *The Rhetoric of Religion* and the totality of Burke's earlier work, Burke's first analogy asks us to read "the supernatural realm allegorically, taking it as the sign of the logic, structure, or order which underlies the empirical" (36).

Having made the argument that it is possible to explain the logic, structure, or order of the empirical realm in terms of the logic, structure, or order of the supernatural realm, Burke closes the first analogy with a discussion that appears at first glance to undermine the "words-Word" analogy. He points out, indeed underscores, the fundamental difference between secular and theological discourse. Talk about the empirical realm or "the world of every day experience" (14) is qualitatively different from talk about the supernatural realm. Whereas talk about the natural ("words for things, for material operations, physiological conditions, animality, and the like"), the sociopolitical ("words for social relations, laws, right, wrong, rule and the like"), and the logological ("the realm of dictionaries, grammar, etymology, philology, literary criticism, rhetoric, poetics, dialectics") (14) has a literal reference, talk about the supernatural does not. As Burke puts it, "The supernatural is by definition the realm of the 'ineffable.' And language by definition is not suited to the expression of the 'ineffable.' So our words for [this] realm, the supernatural or 'ineffable,' are necessarily borrowed from our words for the sorts of things we can talk about literally" (15). However, rather than performing a subversion of the words-Word analogy, this qualitative difference prescribes a methodological caution; namely, the logologist must suspend at least provisionally the referential function of language and treat the various linguistic realms as semiological fields whose force is defined not in terms of their content but, rather, in terms of their form.

The second analogy has to do with what Burke calls the matter-spirit relation, the way in which the natural realm (the less-than-verbal) is "pervaded, or *inspirited,* by the realm of the verbal, or symbolic" (17). The analogy starts out by distinguishing the word from the thing it names. Even though the word "itself is material, a 'body,' a meaning 'incarnate' . . . the word's 'meaning' is not identical with its sheer materiality" (16). Likewise, the symbol is not identical to the symbolized: quite as the word "transcends" the thing it names, so too "[t]here is a qualitative difference between the symbol and the symbolized" (16). Here Burke establishes that the force of language is not attributable to its being adequate to an extralinguistic referent or meaning. Instead, its force is rooted in the intralinguistic resources of the figures themselves. It is precisely for this reason that it can be said that language "grace[s] nature" (16), that "the realm of the symbolic corresponds (in our analogy) to the realm of the 'supernatural' " (17).

If the purpose of the first two analogies is, at least in part, to calculate the force of linguistic or symbolic acts, to determine the kind of work they do by contemplating how they operate, the purpose of the third analogy is to try to account for such force by specifying its starting point. On what condition is the historical emergence of symbolic or linguistic action possible? Although a full answer does not come until the sixth and final analogy, something like a thumbnail sketch is provided here. The fundamental condition of the historical emergence of symbolic or linguistic action is certainly, Burke writes, "a feeling for the *principle of the negative*" (18).

To explain the principle of the negative Burke proposes to attend to "the point that the Korzybski school of linguistics stresses so insistently" but that nonetheless "is repeatedly ignored in practice" (17–18). Simply, in order for language to be used properly it "must be 'discounted' " (18). Picking up and extending a point he had made in the introduction to the chapter, Burke explains that "whatever *correspondence* there is between a *word* and the *thing* it names, the word is *not* the thing. The *word* 'tree' is *not* a tree. And just as effects that can be got with the thing can't be got with the word, so effects that can be got with the word can't be got with the thing. But because these two realms coincide so usefully at certain points, we tend to overlook the areas where they radically diverge. We gravitate spontaneously towards naive verbal realism" (18). Not only is the word not the thing, the symbol not the symbolized, but the symbolic per se is also not natural. That is, any word, symbol, or symbolic construct "is purely and simply an expression internal to a specific symbol-system, and not a 'thing' discoverable in nature" (18). This discontinuous relation between the symbolic and the natural or "other-than-symbolic" realms leads Burke to the paradox of the negative that governs all symbol systems and, thus, secures the "words-Word" analogy that is the basis of logological interpretation: "Quite as the word 'tree' is verbal and the *thing* tree is non-verbal, so all words for the non-verbal must, by the very nature of the case, discuss the realm of the non-verbal in terms of *what it is not*. Hence, to use words properly, we must spontaneously have a feeling for the *principle of the negative*" (18). No doubt this principle or paradox of the negative is reminiscent of Burke's paradoxes of substance and consubstantiality that inform *A Grammar of Motives* and *A Rhetoric of Motives*, respectively.[4] Here the same logic is at work but on a different register.

This difference in registers, however, marks a significant turn in preoccupation. Not only does the principle of the negative lend additional credence to the "words-Word" analogy that is the linchpin of logology; it also makes legible a structural possibility broader and more originary than the dialectic—that which was posited in the *Grammar* and the *Rhetoric* as the condition of possibility for the historical emergence of individual and collective being. Whereas the thinking through of the paradox of substance marks Burke's attempt to articulate the ontological foundation of the historical emergence of the human agent (the *is* of individual being), and whereas the thinking through of the notion of consubstantiality marks his attempt to articulate the ontological foundation of the historical emergence of the social (the *is* of collective being), the investigation of the paradox of the negative marks his attempt to articulate "the critical role of the negative principle in all such thinking" and in all such being (22). That is to say, here Burke manages to exceed his prior theorizations of the condition of possibility for the historical emergence of individual as well as of collective being by questioning implicitly what he had earlier taken for granted as an absolute foundation, as a centering, grounding force or principle: the movement of the dialectic. In the *Grammar* the movement of the dialectic was posited as that which makes possible the finessing of the action/motion differential in the human being and, thus, the historical emergence of a self; in the *Rhetoric* the movement of the dialectic guarantees the emergence of the social, the provisional sublation of the individual into the collective. In *The Rhetoric of Religion*, however, Burke accounts for the movement of the dialectic itself and specifies its inaugurating principle. The principle of the negative is more originary than the movement of the dialectic; in fact, it ensures the movement of the dialectic precisely because the dialectic is rooted in it. As Burke argues in his sixth analogy, even Hegelian metaphysics finds its ultimate resources in the principle of the negative: "[M]uch the same sort of structure can be discerned in the Hegelian dialectic. Given the genius of the negative, the term 'thesis' of itself implies 'antithesis'—and both together imply 'synthesis,' the element of communication between them" (30). Thus in distinction to Hegel, Heidegger, and even Bergson from whom he takes his cue, Burke steps behind the "Idea of Nothing" that is for them "the metaphysical ground of being" and recovers out from under it the "Idea of No"—"a kind of *Weltanschauung* that is imperfectly but inescapably operating in all of us" (21). To charge the wholly linguistic and thoroughly rhetorical "Idea of No" with the becoming-present of individual and collective being is indeed a decisive move for Burke and one to which I will return shortly. Let me simply say here that it is the principle of the negative that, as Cary Nelson so aptly expresses, leads to "Burke's tremendously important argument that language is not simply a tool we use as we will but a structured—and hierarchically arrayed—source of motivation," one that encourages us to doubt the notion of the individual human agent as "a free and independently active subject" (170).[5]

It is out of the principle of the negative that Burke derives his fourth, fifth, and sixth analogies. Having established through the principle of the negative that even words for the natural realm always and necessarily perform a transcendence that is, in a manner of speaking, a kind of displacement, Burke argues in his "Titular" analogy on behalf of "the linguistic drive towards a Title of Titles, a logic of entitlement that is completed by thus rising to ever and ever higher orders of generalization" (25).[6] As I noted above, the principle of the negative and the movement it engenders enable Burke to discern a correspondence not only "between negativity in language and its place in negative theology" but between negativity in language and its place in Platonic, Hegelian, and Heideggerian metaphysics as well. The process of entitlement, "which turns out to have this negative principle as an essential part of its character," stresses "the search for a title of titles, an over-all term . . . [a] 'god-term' " (25) that makes visible the principle that unifies a conglomerate of particulars. For example, "Imagine the ideal title of a book. An ideal title would 'sum up' all the particulars of the book. It would in a way 'imply' these particulars. Yet the particulars would have all the material reality. Similarly with a movement towards a title of titles (the unifying principle that is to be found in a sentence, considered as a "title" for the situation it refers to)" (25). Embedded in the movement toward a title of titles, however, is a kind of paradox or doubled significance, for though on the one hand the "god-term" is satiated with meaning, on the other it signifies "a kind of *emptying*." The "god-term" is, as Burke puts it, "a *via negativa*" (25).

What I have called the doubled significance of the process of entitlement feeds into Burke's fifth analogy concerning "the relation between 'time' and 'eternity' " (27) and his sixth analogy analyzing "the relation between the name and the thing named" (34). To specify the role of the principle of the negative in the construction of these last two analogies it is necessary to recall Burke's illustration of the double movement the negative makes possible. He writes as follows:

[T]he fourth [analogy] concerns the nature of language as a process of entitlement, leading in the secular realm towards an over-all title of titles. Such a secular summarizing term would be technically a "god-term," in the sense that its role was analogous to the over-all entitling role played by the theologian's word for the godhead.

Note that we could also view this fourth analogy in reverse direction. That is, instead of looking upon "God" as the title of titles in which all is summed up, one could look at all subclasses as materially "emanating" or "radiating" from this "spiritual source." And thus, just as religion could be viewed as central, with all specialized fields such as law, politics, ethics, poetry, art, etc. "breaking off" from it and gradually becoming "autonomous" disciplines, so there is a technical sense in which all specialization can be treated as radiating from a Logological center. (25–26)

For Burke, one can make visible the underlying principle that informs the production of both the "special idioms" and the "Logological center" by reversing the order. That is, one can treat the summarizing gesture as prior to that which it summarizes and in so doing determine the logic of the unfolding. In similar fashion, Burke argues, one can decipher both the ambiguous relation between "terms for 'temporal' orders" and "terms for 'fixed' orders" (fifth analogy) and the ambiguous relation between "terms for 'logical priority' and terms for 'temporal' priority" (sixth analogy). Here I should like to proceed cautiously since it is in the fifth and sixth analogies that Burke makes explicit the protocols of logological interpretation, which, as I mentioned earlier, takes the essentialization of the temporal as its general rule.

For his fifth analogy Burke takes as his point of departure a quotation from St. Augustine's *Confessions* (a theological text to which an entire chapter of *The Rhetoric of Religion* is devoted) that seeks to come to terms with the transient nature of things. Burke quotes St. Augustine (Book IV, Chapter X) as saying: "Thus much hast Thou given them, because they are parts of things, which exist not all at the same time, but by departing and succeeding they together make up the universe, of which they are parts. And even thus is our speech accomplished by signs emitting a sound; but this, again, is not perfected unless one word pass away when it has sounded its parts, in order that another may succeed it" (27). Out of St. Augustine's theological speculations evolves Burke's logological proposition that what speech betrays in its phonetic movement is the inconsequentiality of temporality itself. Meaning is produced as sequence gives way to essence. This is indeed the thesis of Burke's fifth analogy: "Here the succession of words in a sentence would be analogous to the 'temporal.' But the *meaning* of the sentence is an *essence*, a kind of fixed significance or definition that is not confined to any of the sentence's parts, but rather pervades or inspirits the sentence as a whole. Such meaning, I would say, is analogous to 'eternity' " (27). For Burke as for St. Augustine meaning exceeds, indeed is other than, the temporal or diachronic series of signs through which it is communicated. "In contrast with the flux of the sentence, where each syllable arises, exists for a moment, and then 'dies' to make room for the next stage of the continuing process, the meaning is 'non-temporal,' though embodied (made incarnate) in a temporal series" (27). Whereas the material appearance of meaning in language and in speech takes place on the trajectory of becoming, "meaning in its unity or simplicity 'just *is*' " (27).

Without a doubt Burke's "Time-Eternity" analogy faithfully reproduces the Appearance/Thing polarity that is associated with Romantic idealism. Following through the notion of the "Time-Eternity" analogy in the interpretation of symbolic acts, Burke provides an additional illustration that virtually announces his indebtedness to this metaphysics:

Recall, for instance, the episode of the Cheshire Cat [of *Alice in Wonderland*]. It smiles. That is, so far as sheer *appearances* are concerned, certain motions, postures and the like take place, and these are interpreted as the signs of a smile. The smile is the *essence* of these material conditions, the *form* or *act* of the sheer motions. It is what the motions "mean." Then the cat disappears, all but its smile. The smile's "temporal" aspects vanish, leaving but their *essence*, their *meaning*. . . . "Smiliness" is not picturable; the closest we can come is to picture one particular smile, by the use of elements that in themselves are *not* smile. These would correspond to the merely "temporal" aspect of the smile's "eternal essence" or meaning that "transcends" any of the visible details. (28)

Translated into narrative temporality, the material appearance of "smiliness" in the Cheshire Cat bespeaks "an entity that can be said to be identical with itself and that would engender, through a process of mediation, an appearance of which it is the origin and the foundation" (de Man 90). That is to say, "smiliness" (the thing proper to which there belongs no temporal determinant—it simply *is*) makes its appearance in and by way of the Cheshire Cat (the metaphor or mode of appearance that is temporally bound—it appears and *then* disappears). Indeed, Burke's own example functions in accordance to the logic of the Appearance/Thing polarity that is traditionally understood "in linguistic terms as the relationship between figural and proper meaning in a metaphor" (de Man 90). The Cheshire Cat is not *really* the entity it literally means, but it points to something ("smiliness") in which meaning and being coincide. Thus the figural, the symbolic, that which necessarily "involves a feeling for the discount," is treated as the play of form and association to which there corresponds a "prior" essence or ground. In short, the use of linguistic elements that are not in themselves the essence for which they stand in "correspond[s] to the merely 'temporal' aspect" of the " 'eternal essence' or meaning that 'transcends' any of the visible details" (28).

Both the figural (Cheshire Cat) and the linguistic (sentence) illustrations used by Burke to establish the priority of the essential over and against the temporal receive support from the sixth and final analogy to which I have already referred. This analogy, which "concerns a notable likeness between the design of the Trinity and the form underlying the 'linguistic situation' " (29), opens with a recuperative gesture. Burke retrieves the distinction between "a *word* and the *thing* it names" that was the empirical basis for his notion of "discount" and the principle of the negative. However, far from being a mere repetition, Burke's rehabilitation and particular mobilization of the distinction here shows that something else is at stake. He writes, "Think first of the relation between the thing and its name (between a tree and the word 'tree'). The power is primarily in the thing, in the tree rather than in the word for tree. But the word is related to this power, this thing, as 'knowledge' about that thing. Hence, derivatively, it has a kind of power, too (the power that is in knowledge, in accurate naming)" (29). I do not read this passage as prefiguring either what some critics have called the vanguard of poststructuralist epistemology or the Foucaultian power-knowledge problematic.[7] To the contrary, the movement of the argument implies the persistence rather than the undoing of a metaphysics of presence and the reaffirmation rather than the denigration of ontology, for what is being proposed here is that truth is accessible. The possession of truth is a matter of correct names since "[q]uite as the first person of the Trinity is said to 'generate' the second, so the thing can be said to 'generate' the word that names it, to call the word into being (in response to the thing's primary reality, which calls for a name)" (29). Given that "the first moment (the thing) provide[s] the ground for the second moment (the name)" (30), a certain "correspondence" obtains between the thing and name, "both together imply 'synthesis,' the element of communication between them" (30). Since "the word for perfect communion between *persons* is 'Love,' " this "technical *cor-*

respondence between thing and name," Burke argues, "would have as its theologic analogue the 'Love' between the First and Second Persons" (30).

At this point in the analogy Burke's argument takes an important but not inconsistent turn. He states the following:

> Since Hegelian metaphysics is so close to theology, much the same sort of structure can be discerned in the Hegelian dialectic. Given the genius of the negative, the term "thesis" of itself implies "antithesis"—and both together imply "synthesis," the element of communication between them. At this point one might object: "But the Hegelian 'antithesis' is *antagonistic* to 'thesis,' whereas the Son, as the Word, is rather in a 'like-father-like-son relationship.' " (30)

In response to this hypothetical challenge Burke revisits the Christian narrative and the Hegelian morphology. He attempts to dispel the suggestion that a discontinuous relation obtains between narrative and logical models of priority. He does so, interestingly enough, not by bringing to the Christian narrative and the Hegelian morphology a grander meaning structure that makes it possible to detect an underlying continuity between them. Instead, Burke dwells "on the interrelationships among the three terms of the Trinity" themselves in order to show that Christian theology itself declares the diachronic, successive structure upon which its story is constructed as illusory. He writes:

> The ambiguous relation between the two styles of placement (the narrative and the logical) can be seen if we stop to consider again the way in which the Second Person of the Trinity is said to "proceed" from the First, and the Third from the First and Second. Though we think of a Father as *preceding* a Son in time, and though we conceive of "generation" in temporal terms, orthodox theologians admonish that the process whereby the Father is said to "generate" the Son must *not* be conceived temporally, that Father and Son are one eternally. We might say that the First Person is "prior" to the Second rather in the *logical* sense (as the first premise could be called prior to the second premise of a syllogism). (32)

What the theologians' own discourse declares is that the difference thought to prevail between temporal and logical notions of priority—the former referring to narrative priority or sequence, the latter referring to "a kind of 'simultaneity' "—is based on a misinterpretation, a miscalculation. Succession is in fact the material appearance of logical simultaneity.

It is, of course, important to notice that neither the theologians' nor Burke's revaluation of the relation between temporal and logical structures rewrites a relation of difference as a relation of equivalence. Indeed, there can be little doubt that rather than displacing difference and, thus, regarding the temporal and the logical as iso-nomic, they valorize logical priority. This seems to be Burke's pur-pose in grafting a genetic model of history onto the empirical (rather than supernatural) realm: "Though there is a sense in which a Father precedes a Son, there is also a sense in which the two states are 'si-multaneous'—for parents can be parents only insofar as they have offspring, and in this sense the offspring 'makes' the parent. That is, logically, Father and Son are *reciprocal* terms, each of which implies the other" (32). By way of the genetic perspective, it is possible for Burke to interpret logical priority as something like an absent cause. Although it is nowhere empirically present as an element, although it is not a part of the whole or one of the levels, it is the nonpresent origin that regulates the relationships between all of the elements and all of the levels. As Burke puts it, "the relations among coeternal persons of the Trinity are *translated* into a temporal series, as regards the unfolding of history" (33, emphasis added).

Here Burke's use of the concept-metaphor "translation" is key, not because it works against his argument but, rather, because it punctu-ates it: the valorization of the logical over and against the temporal finds its justification in the absolute privilege of the original. And the original is nothing less than the "Idea of No" that is the sovereign and autonomous beginning: "Hegel, of course, built his theory of his-tory about an ambiguity of the same sort. From the strictly logical point of view, Hegel's history was over before it ever began; the 'Idea' contained all its possibilities from the very start. But the manifesting of this 'Idea' in terms of nature and history was like the gradual re-vealing of these logical implications one by one" (33). Like Hegel's and Joachim of Floris's theories of history and Coleridge's dialectical pentad, Burke's final analogy and logological project in general ad-monishes against the "tendency to assume a simple historical devel-opment" (35). Indeed, it advocates circularity:

[I]f we say that *idea B* is "implicit in" *idea A*, the translation of this relation-ship into terms of temporal sequence brings up a quasi-mystical paradox. For if we begin with *idea A*, and meditate upon it until we find *idea B* implicit in it, then so far as time sequence is concerned *idea B* has followed *idea A*. We have *proceeded in time* in such a way that we went *from A to B*. Yet, insofar as B was implicit there from the start, there is a sense in which its presence in A preceded our discovery of it there. Thus, in another sense, our step forward is rather like a step backwards, like being *reminded* of some-thing. (238)

Cause anticipates effect because in the beginning is inscribed the end. In this sense "to 'discover' [the end] is but to formulate what one somehow knew before one ever began" (238).

A Logological Reading of the Relation of Structure and Subject

Such are Burke's six internally coherent and interanimating analogies out of which, I suggested earlier, a strategy of interpretation is derived. It should be stressed that in taking the six analogies as a reading lesson of sorts I am in no way working against the grain of *The Rhetoric of Religion*. To the contrary, after having discussed each of the analogies Burke declares as much: "It is my notion that, following such cues, we can finally develop a considerable body of conceptual instruments for shifting back and forth between 'philosophic' and 'narrative' terminologies of motives, between temporal and logical kinds of sequence, thereby finding it easy to translate discussions of 'principles' or 'beginnings' back and forth into either of these styles" (33). At this point it should be fairly clear that logological interpretation and "the 'philosophy of language' that is here being presented roundabout" (38) advocate what I and at least one other critic call "the essential[ization of] the temporal" (Melia 66). Since meaning is anterior to and dialectically transcends the chain of signifiers necessary to its expression, the reader can discount temporal succession and instead look to "the 'directionless' way in which a cluster of terms imply one another" (4). As Trevor Melia puts it, the logologist "must abandon the linear narrative in favor of a detemporalized cycle of terms and move from the rhetorical realm of the merely plausible or probable into the realm of terminological necessity"[8] (66–67).

Importantly enough, in answering the question, "What goes with what in this structure of terms?" (Burke 1970, 39), the logologist both uncovers the logic of a text's unfolding and, by analogy, reveals the motive that lies beneath and infuses the sociopolitical order. For, as I noted at the beginning of this chapter, "however the world is made, that is how language is made." Indeed, it is precisely in this way that the logologist supersedes the dramatistic critic: not only does she apprehend man as the symbol-using animal; she also begins to comprehend the motive underlying the development of a sociopolitical order whose demise looms heavy in the distance. That motive that never appears as such, Burke teaches us, is nothing less than "the spirit of hierarchy" (40) inborn to *homo dialecticus*. Thus not only is man the "symbol-using animal," but he is also the political animal—the being proper "moved by a sense of order" (42) that "implicitly contains his end" (257).

It is to reveal the "hierarchical motive" that lies beneath, infuses, and makes its material appearance in the sociopolitical order that Burke logologically interprets the first three chapters of Genesis, itself a story of origins, about the very birth of human history. Mindful "that theology is the ideology of religion and religion is a system of action—specifically, of governance" (Freccero 56),[9] Burke opens the interpretation, importantly enough, with a loose reference to Hobbes's *Leviathan* that "makes us acutely conscious of the Biblical stress upon *Covenants* as motives" (174). Through this notion of the covenant, Burke launches into the problematic that is at the heart of his logological investigation: the relationship between subject and structure. To what extent can the human being intervene in a structure that always and already antedates it? That is to say, if the hierarchic incentive is one of the ontological determinants of man and, thus, a condition of possibility that makes coemergent the historical appearance of the individual and the social, to what extent is it possible to assert that the human being authorizes or is the author of his actions? Cary Nelson catches this notion thus: "Put somewhat baldly, the issue is whether one sees the symbol-using animal . . . as an independent agent or as a figure occupying the role of agency within a verbal drama that is in a sense already written for us" (157). Or, to use William Rueckert's terms, to what extent is human action an "imitating [of] the grammar of ascent inherent in abstraction" (1989, 248), the principle of the negative that governs the movement of the dialectic?

The structure-subject problematic that drives Burke's reading of the first three chapters of Genesis finds its theological or profane equivalent in the question, To what extent was Adam's violation of his covenant with God an act of free will? To begin to formulate an answer to this question, Burke pulls out of the theological story four key narrative events. That is, he reduces the multiplicity of surface details to four essential elements: "Narratively, there was the Creation; then came the 'Edenic' Covenant (which included the injunction against eating of the tree of the knowledge of good and evil); then the Fall; and then the 'Adamic' Covenant (3:14–19) which included punishments for Adam's first disobedience" (175). Having identified a set of seemingly fixed and irreversible episodes that constitute the story, Burke makes the following observation:

[T]hough this order is irreversible from the standpoint of narrative, there is a sense in which we can reverse the order. For instance, we could "begin" with the idea of a punishment; next we could note that the idea of punishment implies the idea of some infraction which makes the punishment relevant; and such infraction implies the need for a set of conditions that make the infraction possible; and insofar as we looked for a "first" set of such conditions, the idea of them would imply the idea of the kind of Creation that allowed for disobedience. (175)

What such a move enables the logologist to detect is the logical priority of the idea of a covenant, the "pre-first" out of which the entire series evolves. Indeed, "[t]o get the point" Burke urges the reader to reflect on Pope's line, "Order is Heaven's first law." How does one interpret, Burke implicitly asks, the term *first* in Pope's formula? "The reader is not quite sure (nor need he be) whether it means first in time, or first in importance, or first in the sense of a logical grounding for all other laws, a kind of 'causal ancestor' from which all other 'laws' could be deduced or derived as lineal descendants" (180). One need not be sure since each in the end necessarily, which is to say logologically, implies the other.

Having "brought out the strategic importance of the part played by the Biblical stress upon the idea of a Covenant" (180), Burke takes a terministic turn. In a manner wholly consistent with the protocols of logological interpretation, he substitutes the term "order" for the term "covenant":

Having no opposite in standard usage, [the term *Covenant*] seems as purely "positive" as words like "stone," "tree" or "table," which are not matched by companion words like "counter-stone," "anti-tree," or "un-table" (except sometimes in the dialectic of E. E. Cummings [sic]). And perhaps the notion of "positive law" secretly contributes to one's feeling that "Covenants" can be treated as "positive," despite the all-importance of the negative in defining the conditions of Adam's fall. The term "Order," on the other hand, clearly reveals its dialectical or "polar" nature, on its face. "Order" implies "disorder," and vice versa. (181)

However, as Burke points out, such a move is not only methodologically legitimate; it is also necessary. The term "order" is "the kind of term we need" because it makes possible the "evol[ution of] a cluster of interrelated key terms" (183) that can serve as the basis for a comparison between the narrative or diachronic style of Genesis and its logological essentialization or synchronic totalization.

It is in the second section of the chapter entitled "Tautological Cycle of Terms for 'Order' " wherein Burke begins to survey the family of terms implicit in the idea of "Order" that the structure-subject problematic is foregrounded as a question concerning the motivation of the "will." The issue is raised in the following manner: "If, by 'Order,' we have in mind the idea of a command, then obviously the corresponding word for the proper response would be 'Obey.' Or, there would be the alternative, 'Disobey.' Thus we have the proportion: Order is to Disorder as Obedience is to Disobedience" (186). Without a doubt, the proportional relation between order-disorder and obedience-disobedience finds its justification in the principle of the negative Burke had outlined in chapter one, and here, too, he recalls an important reservation that had been raised before: namely, "there is a logological sense in which the things of nature could be called 'innocent' " (186). The things of nature, governed absolutely by the laws of motion, do not in any way actively participate in the social order. As is the case in the Biblical myth wherein natural things "can merely do as they were designed to do" (186), natural things unlike human beings in the empirical realm are not subject to sociopolitical sanction.

This distinction between natural things and human beings is crucial for Burke inasmuch as it sets the conditions for an investigation into the subject of human will, morality, and ethics: "[Natural things] cannot disobey commands, since they cannot understand commands. They do not have a 'sense of right and wrong,' or, more generically, a 'sense of yes and no.' They simply do as they do—and that's that. Such would be the *non posse peccare* of natural things, or even of humans insofar as their 'natural' state was not bound by moralistic negatives" (186). In contrast to the forbidden fruit that is mere agency of Adam's fall, Adam himself is agent: "Adam can do even what [he] has been explicitly told not to do. The word-using animal not only understands a thou-shalt-not; it can carry the principle of the negative a step further, and answer the thou-shalt-not with a disobedient No" (186–87).

At this point in the argument it would seem that Burke unequivocally affirms the free will of the human being: whereas " '[t]hings' can but *move* or *be moved* . . . '[p]ersons' by definition can 'act' " (187). Put differently, insofar as human beings are "endowed with words (symbols) by which they can frame responses to questions and commands" (187), they can intervene in structure, exercise choice in a scene.

However, having arrived at this point, Burke detects a watershed moment, the "ultimate riddle": "If order, implying the possibility of disorder, implies a possible *act* of disobedience, then there must be an agent so endowed, or so minded, that such an act is possible to him—and the *motives* for such an act must eventually somehow be referred to the *scene* out of which he arose, and which thus somehow contains the principles that in their way make a 'bad' act possible" (192). Here the "free will" of human being is made indefinite. The structural possibility of the sovereign subject and, thus, the active intervention into structure are compromised: whether the act is understood as a "No-saying" to order or as a "Yea-saying" to a counter-order (counter-covenant), "[p]roblems of 'predestination' lie in the offing" (196). Indeed, "[v]iewed here not as doctrine, but sheerly as design," Hobbes's *Leviathan* (the document to which Burke turns in the third section of this chapter) "helps us realize that [even in the wholly secular realm of sociopolitical organization], implicit in the idea of a Covenant is the idea not just of obedience or disobedience to that Covenant, but also of obedience or disobedience to a *rival* Covenant" (199). Insofar as the "idea" of disobedience to a particular covenant or the obedience to a rival covenant is implicit in the idea of order, there is a sense in which its actualization as human action has already been determined. There is a sense in which, as Trevor Melia puts it, human action must be understood as "symbolic *motion*" (68).

Human action as something that always and already carries within it the trace of motion is not, as I have tried to show in the previous chapters, something new to Burke's theorization of individual and collective action. However, the difference here lies in the suggestion that the motion differential cannot be thought of merely as the other side of the self-same coin. Instead, the motion differential is part and parcel of the action differential; the action differential is itself a doubled structure. Stated logologically,

> whereas narratively the Lord God's thou-shalt-not preceded the serpent's tempting of Eve, by appealing to the imagination, in mixing imagery of food with imagery of rule ("and ye shall be as *Elohim*"), and whereas the tempting preceded the fall, logologically the thou-shalt-not [the condition of possibility for the material appearance of human action] is itself implicitly a condition of temptation, since the negative contains the principle of its own annihilation. For insofar as a thou-shalt-not, which is intrinsic to Order verbally guided, introduces the principle of negativity, here technically is the inducement to round out the symmetry by carrying the same principle of negativity one step farther, and negating the negation. That is the only kind of "self-corrective" the negative as such has. (218–19)

Burke's noticing of the doubled character of human action out of which is produced what he here and elsewhere calls "second nature" (220) brings to the fore a not altogether unanticipated or unrecognizable disjunction between the theological and logological interpretation of the creation myth.[10] Burke writes:

> Though, as we have said, the theological and logological interpretations of Genesis are simply in different planes, so that they neither corroborate nor refute each other, at one point there does seem to be a necessary opposition:
> Theologically, Adam could have chosen *not* to sin. He could have said yes to God's thou-shalt-not.
> But logologically, Adam *necessarily* sinned. (252)

What Burke emphasizes here is that in terms of the Christian narrative, the linear progression of the story leaves open—indeed thematically demands—the possibility of Adam's deciding to respect his covenant with God. It is only by preserving the sovereign human subject that the story has any kind of moral or ethical force and, thus, rhetorical or ideological hold. However, and this is the critical point, from a logological perspective Adam's sin was an "over all terministic 'inevitably.' " By virtue of the principle of the negative, the condition of possibility for human action that "is the inducement to round out the symmetry by carrying the principle of negativity one step farther, and negating the negation," Adam "most certainly *did* 'have to' " sin (253). The act was "de-termined" from the start by the logic of "the Cycle of Terms Implicit in the Idea of 'Order' " (252).

Burke's logological claim that Adam's eating from the tree of knowledge of good and evil must be understood not as the act of a free and self-willing subject but, instead, as an act that makes visible the way in which subjects perform structure is, as I have suggested time and again, in complete harmony with the logic of the Hegelian dialectic from which Burke draws his sixth analogy. In a manner wholly analogous to the Hegelian morphology, Burke's logologic and the principle of the negative upon which it is constituted require a final sublation: Adam had to sin.

It must be emphasized that the discontinuity between the logological and theological interpretations of the Genesis story is not something that evades Burke's comprehension. Quite to the contrary, he himself points to it and draws the complication out. That is to say, Burke attempts neither to finesse nor to cover over this difference. Instead, he underscores it and then proceeds to defend logology as an interpretive strategy that avoids the imagistic reductionism and excessive anthropomorphism inherent in all such mythic accounts (254–65). What is curious, however, is that Burke does so by resorting to generic or narratological analysis. It is to the fixed, irreversible, and irreducible sequence of events that constitute story that Burke appeals in order to assert the priority of logological analysis. He writes:

[L]ogologically, Adam *necessarily* sinned. For if he had chosen *not* to sin, the whole design of the Bible would have been ruined. The fundamental "first," which links Creation with the Fall, and sets up the conditions for Redemption, would be missing. The Pauline logic would have been without a grounding in the Book, since the Book of Beginnings would itself have been without the kind of beginning that sets up the conditions for the tragic sacrifice. The Bible would not have said, in its opening narrative, that man is "in principle" a sinner and thus "in principle" needs a Redeemer, in accordance with the logic of the Cycle of Terms Implicit in the Idea of "Order." (252)

In striking opposition to the genetic model of history presented in chapter one, which sought to dispel the suggestion that a discontinuous relation obtains between narrative and logical modes of priority and to assert the efficacy of a strategy of interpretation that takes "circularity" as its rule, what is now being pressed is the absolute necessity of a "first" *in time.* Adam must have sinned in order for the Redemption *to follow.* As Burke puts it, "The Bible would thus [otherwise] have lacked the formal 'felicity' of the Fall (the *felix culpa* that brought about the coming of Christ)" (252). Here Burke has clearly shifted from the logical to the temporal mode of priority. The discussion is overtly punctuated by words having temporal rather than spatial connotations: "brought about," "coming of," "sets up the conditions for." Etymologically, even the concept-metaphor "felicity" connotes a sense of the timely, the appropriate, that which arises not out of logical necessity but, rather, out of temporal urgency.

The claim that Burke's defense of the logological interpretation of the creation myth exceeds its own protocols by seeking validation in narrative diachrony itself finds additional support in the brief discussions of Milton's *Paradise Regained* and Shakespeare's *Othello* that immediately follow. About *Othello* Burke writes: "Logologically, to say that Adam didn't have to sin would be like saying that Oedipus didn't have to kill his father and sleep with his mother, except that in the case of Adam it *looks* like more of a choice. Or it's like saying that Othello 'didn't have to' kill Desdemona. As regards the logic of the fable, the formal requirements of tragedy, he most certainly *did* 'have to.' The act is 'de-termined' by the symmetry of the terms as a whole. He *necessarily* had to kill her, in order that the play be a tragedy" (252–53). At this particular juncture Burke is appealing neither to the "directionless circularity of terms" nor to the necessary movement of the dialectic toward a final and predetermined sublation born out of the principle of the negative. Rather, what he is enlisting is a theory of genre that determines the identity of the text on the basis of the *sequence* of events that constitute plot.[11] Essentially, Burke argues that if, as in the case of tragedy, the fatal blow does not take place, another *sequence* of events must necessarily follow. The preemption of the cataclysmic event signifies the presence of an altogether different form. Thus for Burke to argue that the first three chapters of Genesis, like a Shakespearean tragedy, must consist of a particular series of events in order for the text to qualify as a member of a given genre is, in the final analysis, to argue in terms of narrative diachrony itself.

Although it is brief, nowhere is Burke's transgression of the protocols of logological interpretation more apparent than when he invokes the example of Milton's *Paradise Regained* as a means for valorizing logological over theological interpretation. Had Adam not sinned, Burke argues, the creation myth "would have been as weak as Milton's *Paradise Regained,* which actually is the account of an initial *refusal* to be tempted (when Christ says 'No' to the tempter's attempts to get him to say 'Yes' to the proposal to say no to God's thou-shalt-not)" (252). Here Burke's own example does not support the claim that it is logically impossible to write a narrative wherein Adam says "yes" to God's thou-shalt-not. Indeed, *Paradise Regained* is, to put it crudely, proof that it can in fact be done. Instead, what this example suggests is that the rhetorical force of the story would have dwindled had the story been constructed that way. Thus it becomes possible for us to say that what Adam's sin performs within the creation story is not a logological but, rather, a *rhetorical* necessity. At the beginning of this chapter I pointed out that the declared secular aim of *The Rhetoric of Religion: Studies in Logology* is to defer a future-present, to keep that which has appeared on the horizon of human history at a distance. I also argued that the first chapter of the book can be read as a lesson of sorts that offers us "a considerable body of conceptual instruments" that make possible the first step toward realizing that goal: namely, to appreciate the origin and logic out of which the present "quandaries of human governance" arise. If, however, as I have argued, *The Rhetoric of Religion: Studies in Logology* contains within itself a moment that makes legible the limits of logological interpretation and, thus, of the dramatistic project in general, can we read these texts as anything other than, as Derrida puts it, "the system of a writing and of a reading which we know is ordered around its own blind spot" (1976, 164)? The task of the final chapter is to answer this question in the affirmative by way of a deconstructive return to Burke's principle of the negative.

5

From Communicative Action to Rhetorical Invention

The turn toward and deconstruction of Burke's trivium of motives, as I stated at the outset of this book, emerge out of the need for a retheorization of the relation of subject and structure and, hence, of social change that makes it possible for us not only to newly appreciate our past but also, and perhaps more important, to refigure a future that is not simply a future-present. Such a task is, without a doubt, as pressing as it is daunting since the very desire to retheorize the conditions of possibility for a transformation of social relations today, *in* our day, is at once both inaugurated and confounded by the vulgarities of what Jean-François Lyotard has summarily termed our "postmodern condition": that "state of affairs" characterized by the "widespread apprehension that the 'old' forms of collectivity are disappearing or have already disappeared, that impersonality, anonymity, and solitude are the lot of a modern humanity crowded into ever-expanding urban conglomerates, that the very bonds of social interaction are sundered by the multifarious dislocations, disruptions and disappropriations that characterize life in postindustrial societies" (Abbeele, x). On the one hand, then, it is out of our deeply troubled relation to the perpetual upheavals within and relentless splinterings of our contemporary lifeworld—upheavals and splinterings that undermine every certainty and underscore the incompleteness of every meaning and every position—that the felt need for a retheorization of the social emerges. On the other hand, the very pro-liferation of those incommensurate and all too often inimical socio-cultural, political, and ethnic differences seems to announce the radi-cal impossibility of an efficacious retheorization of collective life and social transformation. Hence, one sees the impossible double bind out of which the social and rhetorical theorist must write today, *in "our"* day, a day in which the anxiety of influence seems to have given way to the psychoneuroses of insularity.

But if, as I am trying to suggest, our lived relation to the post-modern is best understood not so much as a *condition* handed over to us but, instead, as an impossible *evocation* to which "we" must re-spond, how are "we" theorists to do so? That is to say, if, as Jean-Luc Nancy has so aptly and passionately written, "the gravest and most painful testimony of the modern world, the one that possibly involves all other testimonies to which this epoch must answer (by virtue of some unknown decree or necessity, for we bear witness also to the exhaustion of thinking through History), is the testimony of the dis-solution . . . or the conflagration of community" (1), how are "we" to find a beginning, a point from which to start? Most certainly not in the "I" understood in terms of an internal self-consciousness that is Cartesian (individualistic), Kantian (intersubjective), or Hegelian (transubjective or world-historical), for what "we" have learned from poststructuralism, if anything, is to break our habit of thinking of the subject or autonomous individual as the community's or collec-tive's organizing category, to guard vigilantly against our trained pro-clivity to conceptualize the social from the notion of "the individual who *then* encounters 'others' " (Abbeele, xii). As a matter of fact, and as I suggested in the opening chapter of this book, it is in the decisive move away from subjectivity and to positionality that the genius of post-Enlightenment or antifoundationalist attempts to refigure the relations of structure and subject is registered. In this view, *to be*—to come into subjectivity, to become a self, or to move into the space of the "I" of enunciation—has the transitive value of a positioning over and against the ontological status of an unveiling. Put a bit differ-ently, in this view the sovereign or self-positing subject is displaced by a notion of identity as wholly or irreducibly relational: the self is only given by its structural position within a larger field of discursive forces or symbolic practices, the totality of which is indeterminable yet determining. At this juncture "we" must proceed with caution, however, since the scenario of the decentered subject is as potentially disabling as it has been enabling. That is to say, "we" must not move too quickly since a retheorization of the social that takes as its point of departure an "I" understood as a contingent articulation or effect structure can all too easily lead "us" down two equally disastrous paths: on the one hand, in presupposing a subject that is an effect of the play of forces operative at a *particular* sociohistorical and cultural moment, "we" run the risk of reducing history to its synchronic totalization; on the other hand, in positing a subject that is an effect of forces that are, as was suggested above, indeterminate yet *determining*, "we" hazard the reinstallation, albeit in clandestine fashion, of a conception of History as the great unmoved mover. In both cases, of course, "we" potentially strip the subject of positive agency, divest "ourselves" of the capacity to act, to invent.

The precise character of the contribution of Burke's work toward an efficacious retheorization of collective life and social transformation in postmodernity can best be discerned by placing it in relation to Jürgen Habermas's elaborate theorization of a "universal pragmatics." Without a doubt, Habermas's universal pragmatics is one of the late twentieth century's most provocative and highly acclaimed attempts to construct a theory of social relations and human emancipation that aims to be at once antiessentialist, mindful of history, cognizant of the complexities that constitute the postmodern predicament, and protective of human agency. As Thomas McCarthy has put it in what is considered by many to be the most masterful and comprehensive analysis of Habermas's work to date: "[Habermas's] critical social theory is empirical without being reducible to empirical-analytic science; it is philosophical but in the sense of critique and not of first philosophy; it is historical without being historicist; and it is practical, not in the sense of possessing a technological potential but in the sense of being oriented to enlightenment and emancipation" (126). Seeking to negotiate the treacherous course between the one and the many, between unity and plurality, between structure and subject—the theme that, as Habermas rightly insists, has governed metaphysics from its inception and that, in the context of the fragmenting effects of societal modernization, returns with more than a modicum of vengeance and renewed relevance as the ethical-political problematic of our age—this second-generation Frankfurt School theorist advances a procedural concept of communicative reason "that is skeptical and postmetaphysical, yet not defeatist" (Habermas 1992, 116). By anchoring his theory in the experiential context of the postmodern lifeworld and finding in the to-and-fro of everyday communicative practices the instantiation, albeit always imperfect, of a dialogical model of intersubjective exchange out of which mutual understanding may emerge, Habermas clears the way for "a concept of situated reason that is given voice in validity claims that are both context-dependent and transcendent" (1992, 139). Indeed it is Habermas's overall project to demonstrate that a procedural concept of communicative reason makes it possible for us to both steer ourselves clear of the unitary thinking of metaphysics and its concomitant idealism and avoid the ludic perspectivism that, in his view at least, is always the accomplice of the more recent radical contextualism put forth by Lyotard, Rorty, Laclau and Mouffe, and others. In short, if "[t]he occlusion of the ability to say 'we' " is, as Calvin Schrag has written and I have suggested above, "the principal chink in the political armor of the new politics of postmodernism" (129–30), Habermas's task is to demonstrate that our best hope for its repair lies in his universal pragmatics.

Habermas's Universal Pragmatics

It is no minor matter that Habermas finds in speech act theory the point of departure for his universal pragmatics and the philosophy of communication that underwrites it. In his view, what is of particular value in speech act theory derives from its founding impulse: to propose a philosophy of language that does not begin with the felicitous assumption that the analysis of "the uses of expressions in speech situations" and the study of "the meaning of sentences" are discrete, indeed competing, forms of inquiry. As J. R. Searle explains:

A typical question in the second approach is, "How do the meanings of the elements of a sentence determine the meaning of the whole sentence?" A typical question in the first approach is, "What are the different kinds of speech acts speakers perform when they utter expressions?" Answers to both questions are necessary to a complete philosophy of language, and more importantly, the two questions are necessarily related. They are related because for every possible speech act there is a possible sentence or set of sentences the literal utterance of which in a particular context would constitute a performance of that speech act. (19)

A thoroughgoing analysis and, hence, understanding of language simply cannot be had if sentences are abstracted from their use in a context, if the propositional content and the illocutionary force of utterances are thought to operate a space apart from one another, if the performative aspect of human utterance drops out of the calculation. In other words, the virtue of speech act theory over and against, for example, generative grammar (wherein the universal structures of speech are at issue), Chomskian linguistics (wherein the underlying competence of the speaker-hearer is analyzed at the expense of other nongrammatical factors), and even Derridean grammatology (wherein the cachet of the graphematic structure is purchased at the price of the subject[1]) is that it vigilantly refuses to disavow or even treat as subsidiary the extralinguistic and pragmatic know-how that speakers mobilize in the act of communicating with others. Thus although the capacity to produce and decipher the locutionary force of sentences is necessary to communicative action, it is by no means the sufficient condition of it. As McCarthy notes in a passage that seeks to briefly summarize Habermas's productive appropriation of speech act theory, requisite to communication is also "the ability to establish and understand those modes of communication and connections with the external world through which speech in ordinary language becomes possible" (276). Speakers must have at their disposal more than a command of the language, they must be able to do more than merely produce sentences that are syntactically and grammatically correct or semantically meaningful; as Habermas states it, they must also be capable of operating within "that fundamental system of rules that adult subjects master to the extent that they can fulfill *the conditions for a happy employment of sentences in utterances,* no matter to which particular language the sentences may belong and in which accidental contexts the utterances may be embedded" (1979a, 26). One of the primary tasks of universal pragmatics, then, is to specify this "pretheoretical" but practically mastered knowledge and to reveal the general or universal conditions of possibility for reaching understanding in ordinary language communication.

Hence, moving along the theoretical vector opened up by speech act theory and, thus, taking the act of utterance or statement rather than the sentence as the basic unit of analysis, Habermas claims that in any instance in which language is deployed for the purpose of communication a crucial set of relations is operative: the first relation is between that which is stated and an extralinguistic reality of phenomena to which the statement refers; the second is between that which is stated and the speaker's own intentional experiences; and the third is between that which is stated and the intersubjectively established values and norms that constitute the shared lifeworld. However, since a speaker may or may not utter truthful statements about the world, may or may not be forthright about his or her intentions, and may or may not produce discourses that respect the shared values and norms or roles and rules of the lifeworld, communicative understanding hinges on the speaker's preparedness, indeed willingness, to hold himself or herself accountable to four different validity claims that are, in most instances, left implicit:

In addition to the claim that what he utters is comprehensible (grammatical in the linguistic sense), the speaker also claims that what he states is true (or, if no statement is made, that the existential presuppositions of his utterance's propositional content are fulfilled); that his manifest expression of intentions is truthful (or veracious: *wahrhaftig*); and that his utterance (his speech *act*) itself is right or appropriate (*richtig/angemessen*) in relation to a recognized normative context (or that the normative context it satisfies is itself legitimate). (McCarthy 280)

In short, communicative understanding becomes a real possibility if and only if all four validity claims are upheld, for it is only under these conditions that listeners can comprehend the speaker's utterance, share fully in the speaker's knowledge, trust the speaker, and reciprocally acknowledge the legitimacy of the underlying norms of the shared lifeworld.

Although the rational reconstruction of "the dialogue constitutive universals . . . [that] establish in the first place the form of intersubjectivity between any competent speakers capable of mutual understanding" (Habermas 1970b, 140) is granted theoretical priority within Habermas's overall project, it most certainly does not constitute its ultimate horizon. As I pointed out early in this chapter, the aspiration is not simply to advance a theory of dyadic or interpersonal communication wherein the possibility of intersubjective understanding is an effect of the speaking process itself, but also, and more important, to extract from the everyday practices of discursive exchange a theory of communicative rationality that can move us collectively toward a more just society, one based on rationally secured right rather than on unwarranted political might. Obviously, in having said this much Habermas burdens himself with the prodigious task of distinguishing the unequivocable difference between the two.

It is news to no one to say that in Habermas's view the constitutive difference between a just and an unjust society is, to borrow the terms from one of his early books, that the former is steered by "knowledge" whereas the latter is operated by "interest." Importantly enough, what Habermas is suggesting is that, even in light of the relatively recent deconstruction of a Western metaphysics of presence and, thus, however tempting it may be to do so, notions such as objectivity and validity cannot be discarded if the possibility for a just society is to remain open; that there is an intimate, indeed necessary, connection between the well-formed or equitable society and knowledge or truth; and that the very notion of social justice as such is unthinkable without some operative conception of truth. But what exactly does Habermas mean by the term "truth"? In making it the centerpiece of his universal pragmatics, is Habermas positioning himself in bold opposition to what can now be taken as nothing less than a formidable tradition of continental thought that has radically undermined the self-presence and transparency of concepts like truth, knowledge, identity, being, and reality? Is he striving to resurrect, in however subtle a manner, a logocentrism that, at best, is regarded by most of his contemporaries as suspect? While it would be preposterous to read Habermas as simply lending his voice to a considerable chorus of praise for deconstruction, it would be equally inane to figure his relation to it in terms of a pure and simple antagonism. Habermas himself has credited "the critique of the philosophy of consciousness" with "pav[ing] the way for postmetaphysical thinking" (1992, 44), and, like many of his contemporaries, he puts no stock in a pre-poststructuralist conception of truth that banks on either an a priority of experience or a priori forms of intuition and categories of understanding. While Habermas writes at considerable length about the mistaken attempts to ground knowledge in experience or the transcendental ego, suffice it to say here that according to him "the objectivity of experience guarantees not the *truth* of a corresponding statement, but the *identity* of experience in the various statements interpreting that experience" (1973, 180), and the interpretation of experience cannot be understood "as the self-realization of an independently acting subject carried out in isolation and freedom but as a linguistically mediated process of socialization" (1992, 152–53). Indeed, lest his work be prematurely discounted, what must be emphasized is that his is a *transformed* conception of truth that both flies in the face of the circular, closed-off structure of unifying reason (logocentrism) and repudiates the celebration of the resolutely contradictory and conflictual (contextualism). The question is, of course, how transformed?

The first step Habermas takes toward a transformed conception of truth is to reject both semantic and correspondence theories of it. On the one hand, by fixing their analytic gaze exclusively on the sentence, semanticists fail to take into consideration the performative component of any assertion and hence foreclose the very possibility of our attaining an understanding of truth. In other words, when it comes to settling the question of the truth or falsity of a constative utterance, we cannot expect to hit upon an answer by merely assessing its propositional content. The pragmatic, which is to say, intersubjectively constituted and constitutive, conditions under which it is possible to justifiably assert the utterance must also be taken into account. To do anything less is to render truth a thoroughly subjective matter: truth is what any given individual claims it might be. As Habermas writes, "the certainty of perception, the paradigm for certainties generally, always holds only for the perceiving subject and for no one else. Of course several subjects can share the certainty that they have a certain perception; but in that case they must say so, i.e. make the same assertion" (McCarthy 301). On the other hand, the remedy for the radical subjectivism that is the unavoidable and insufferable consequence of a semantic theory of truth is not to be found in an alternative theorization that gauges the truth value of a constative utterance exclusively on the basis of a perceived correspondence or lack thereof between its propositional content and an extralinguistic reality to which it refers. According to Habermas, correspondence theories of truth do not cut the mustard for the simple reason that far from settling the question of the relation between truth value and intersubjective recognition they beg it by failing to realize that the "reality" or "facts" to which a given assertion is said to correspond are no less a matter of predication than the asserting itself. McCarthy sums up in the following way Habermas's considerable dissatisfaction with a long history of philosophical attempts to propose a "reality check" as the test of truth:

[T]he "correspondence" of statements with facts is not a correspondence between linguistically structured statements and a linguistically naked reality-in-itself. A statement p is true if it is indeed the case that (or a fact that) p. Both terms of the relation belong to "the sphere of language"—"the fact that p," has the same categorical structure as p. This is not to say that statements are (or rather need be) *about* language. What a statement is about is determined by its denotative component. Thus statements are about (or may be about) "things or happenings on the face of the globe." But what they state is "that" the thing or event referred to possesses the properties, features, and relations predicatively ascribed to it. And operations of predication, no less than those of denotation, are operations in language. They are successful at one level if the governing conventions of the language in question are properly observed. They are successful at another level if the language itself is appropriate or adequate to the object domain under consideration. As our theory languages change and develop, so too does our stock of available statements *and facts*. (302)

In the final analysis, then, Habermas regards both semantic and correspondence theories of truth as untenable.

If the first step Habermas takes toward a transformed conception of truth is discrediting prior theorizations of it, his next step is to advance a viable alternative of his own. "Communicative rationality" is the name Habermas assigns to his revamped consensus theory of truth, which proposes that the truth value of a claim can be ascertained only by way of an intersubjective rational-critical debate that interrogates not the constative utterance per se but the viability of the reasons that warrant its assertability. In other words, as William Mark Hohengarten has written:

Habermas argues that, in general, we evaluate truth claims not by directly comparing a statement with a state of affairs in the objective world but by examining the *reasons* that a speaker can give in support of what she says. Claiming that one's statement is true, or valid, is tantamount to claiming that good reasons can be given in support of it. In Habermas's words: "The speaker refers with his validity claim to a potential of reasons that could be brought to bear for it." These reasons are in turn evaluated in terms of their *intersubjective* acceptability as good reasons for holding something to be the case. (x)

The true statement is, then, a claim that has been or potentially can be argumentatively vindicated and, thus, merits the agreement of all. However, as the preceding recapitulation of Habermas's position already indicates, he does not naively pin all his hopes for the ascension to truth on the discourse that is or can be ushered in support of a claim. Truth is a thoroughly intersubjective affair, and, hence, the force of "the better argument" cannot carry the day if the day already belongs to or is already operated by any motive, witting or not, other than the cooperative search for truth. Because the truth can set us free only when the intersubjective conditions are set for it to do so, Habermas advances his by now famous "ideal speech situation," which gives universal-pragmatic characterization to the mode of redemption of truth claims requisite to the unfolding of a genuine consensus. At once a hypothetical characteristic or future possibility and something that already is immanent or anticipated in all communicative practice, the ideal speech situation specifies the protocols of a form of discursive exchange in which "communication [is] uninhibited by inequalities of status and power" (Lee 415) and, thus, one out of which an interest-free and resolutely rational consensus may emerge. The linchpin of the ideal speech situation or of what Thomas Farrell has described as the " 'original condition', [or] norm of interaction to which false consciousness and closed speech must finally submit" (191) is, of course, Habermas's symmetry thesis:

This freedom from internal and external constraint can be given a universal-pragmatic characterization; there must be for all participants a symmetrical distribution of chances to select and employ speech acts, that is, an effective equality of chances to assume dialogue roles. If this is not the case, the resultant agreement is open to the charge of being less than rational, of being the result not of the force of the better argument but, for example, of open or latent relations of domination, of conscious or unconscious strategic motivations. Thus the idea of truth points ultimately to a form of interaction that is free from all distorting influences. The "good and true life" that is the goal of critical theory is inherent in the notion of truth; it is anticipated in every act of speech. (McCarthy 308)

Cleansed of any privilege, interlocutors meet on a thoroughly leveled discursive playing field whose regulative ideal is "may the best argument win."

That some rhetorical and argumentation theorists remain enthusiastic about Habermas's universal pragmatics should come as no surprise, for as the foregoing summary illustrates, Habermas not only operationalizes the god-terms or buzz words intimately associated with that fraternity of scholars; like them, he also takes the art of deliberation to be the key to understanding the limits and possibilities of collective life, the potentially positive noncoercive lever through which social transformation and, ultimately, human freedom are to be realized. Indeed, according to Habermas a certain kind of practice of deliberation, namely, "the communicative employment of propositional knowledge in assertions" over and against "the noncommunicative employment of knowledge in teleological action" (1984, 10), is that which opens the way for systematic critique and, thus, inaugurates the formation of a collective rational will to social evolution. As Habermas puts it in a passage that explicitly and without the slightest sense of apprehension acknowledges the pivotal role of argument in the reshaping of society:

[I]f we start from the communicative employment of propositional knowledge in assertions, we make a prior decision for a wider concept of rationality connected with ancient conceptions of *logos*. This concept of *communicative rationality* carries with it connotations based ultimately on the central experience of the unconstrained, unifying, consensus-bringing force of argumentative speech, in which different participants overcome their merely subjective views and, owing to the mutuality of rationally motivated conviction, assure themselves of both the unity of the objective world and the intersubjectivity of their lifeworld. (1984, 10)

From out of the give and take of propositional knowledge put forward by a multiplicity of interlocutors whose driving motive is understanding rather than instrumental mastery emerges a consensus that carries within it the action-bearing force of a "we," "a unity of reason" that, as Habermas explains by way of Gadamerian hermeneutics, signifies not the mere "assimilation to 'us' " but, rather, a "merging of interpretive horizons" or a "convergence, steered through learning, of 'our' perspective *and* 'their' perspective" (1992, 138). Hence, by renouncing any and all metaphysical trumps and reconceiving the very possibility of the (re)formation of a collective will in the postmodern age as the immanent, albeit yet to be rendered manifest, product of rational discursive exchange, Habermas not only one-ups the transition from the philosophy of consciousness to the philosophy of language by way of a philosophy of communication. More important, for rhetorical and argumentation theorists at least, he also and at the same time grants to the art of deliberation a privileged position within that new philosophy.

If what rhetorical and argumentation theorists were hoping to find in Habermas was not just a sympathetic ear for their own work but an intellectual force that would incontrovertibly secure its rightful status within the human sciences, they have surely been disappointed, for contrary to their expectations and Habermas's own intentions, universal pragmatics has not, generally speaking, moved readers to admit the centrality and redemptive power of rational deliberation for postmodernity but, instead, has induced them to expose its limited relevance to the task of addressing the critical social and political exigencies that vex human existence in the late twentieth century. Indeed, Habermas's universal pragmatics (and likewise the ideal speech situation whose possibility is grounded in the fundamental rationality of communication) is often discounted for being little more than the dreamy-eyed speculation of a nostalgic utopianist vainly seeking to realize the untapped potential of the bourgeois conception of the public sphere. Like other critics who are more than a bit skeptical about Habermas's claim that it is possible to overcome the inequities and injustices of the present by dipping into and renovating selected Enlightenment tenets of the past, Jane Flax has written:

Many of us find quite appealing [the] promise of the existence of a neutral yet emancipatory reason, an undetermined subject, and a progressive and ultimately benign logic to history. The possibilities that the exercise of authority could be innocent of domination and that political life can be a rational and harmonious coordination of autonomous self- and other-regarding beings have tremendous appeal. I would like to believe them myself.

However, I cannot. . . .

There are no transhistorical or neutral justifications of the views a particular social arrangement favors. No epistemological procedures exist that can cleanse our knowledge of its multiple origins, or prohibit the effects that escape our intentions and think us as we think we are mastering them. Any form of knowledge is a product and reflection of human wishes and practices, including the will to power. The availability of certain kinds of knowledge is as much a matter of contingency, the available struggles for power, and the history of past and present practices as it is of the triumph of truth over error.

The temporary privilege of some views over others will be a consequence of a variety of factors, including power struggles and the wielding of truth claims. (30–31)

For critics like Flax, Mansbridge, Eley, and others, a critical theory that founds the possibility of the abolition of domination on the acquiescence of all potential participants to a set of argumentative protocols whose function is to bar private interests and inequalities of status and, thus, promote unrestricted rational discussion is counterfactual and, hence, politically and historically naive. The complexities of power and interest simply cannot be dispensed with so easily. Indeed, according to these readers, Habermas's universal pragmatics is objectionable not simply because the proposed normative rules for discursive exchange cannot manage to thoroughly bracket out privilege and power but also, and perhaps more importantly as Nancy Fraser suggests, because those protocols surreptitiously usher them in and in so doing militate against progressive social change. As she puts it, "Insofar as the bracketing of social inequalities in delibera-tion means proceeding as if they do not exist when they do, this does not foster participatory parity. On the contrary, such bracketing usu-ally works to the advantage of dominant groups in society and to the disadvantage of subordinates" (11). Quite simply stated, according to these critics Habermas's conception of an ideal form of argument that presumably shelves economic and political inequalities as well as cultural differences on behalf of promoting understanding holds little promise and packs little punch for those members of the post-modern *polis* who have most to gain from the transformation of social relations. In this view, universal pragmatics is both counter-factual and counterproductive.

To say that Habermas's universal pragmatics is counterproductive is one thing; to say it is counterfactual and then reject it on the basis of its utopianism is quite another. For although I want to agree with these critics that Habermas's commitment to the articulation of a set of argumentative protocols whose purpose is to make it possible for interlocutors to "overcom[e] the historical or agonistic differences that keep them from being at one with themselves, that keep them from being themselves" (Abbeele, xii) works against his own desire for progressive social change (albeit for somewhat different reasons that I will come to shortly), I also believe with Thomas Farrell that there is an important sense in which those critics who impatiently dismiss Habermas's universal pragmatics for its utopianism "miss the point." As Farrell has put it, correctly I think:

A great many of the questions which have been directed toward the plausi-bility and coherence of this ideality notion seem to ignore the inescapability of some such counterfactual ideal as an impartial standard grounding all in-vestigatory and demonstrative argument (such as formal and symbolic logic, mathematics and calculus, and whatever remains of philosophy). Habermas, well aware of the irony of origins, is reminding us that not just *any* set of circumstances is sufficient to produce the consensus on validity claims which make communicative action intelligible. Moreover, the absence of such a consensus *in fact* does not remove the possibility of such a consensus under optimal conditions. This is the major thrust of Habermas's argument. Questions about whether such a utopian setting could ever be attained his-torically also miss the point. For the point is that Habermas has offered at least a plausible candidate for a standard, one that avoids the problems of infinite regress and relativism that have plagued consensus theory. (192)

As Farrell points out, Habermas is neither unaware of the fact that rational communicative action is the exception rather than the norm nor oblivious to the fact that although "[o]ur first sentence expresses unequivocally the intention of universal and unconstrained consensus" (McCarthy 287), communicative understanding is rarely the motive for or outcome of discursive exchange. Nonetheless, because communicative understanding is immanent in all speech acts it can be extrapolated into an ideal and taken up as a vantage point from which to critique the vast majority of discourses that deviate from or fall short of it.

Despite his largely sympathetic reading of Habermas, however, Farrell is not altogether satisfied with universal pragmatics. But as I have already noted, the significant shortcoming of universal pragmatics is not, in his view, the ideal speech situation, for "[a]s long as we know this to be a postulated, counterfactual condition, then we can get along in real speech situations, what Bitzer calls *rhetorical* situations, without serious difficulty" (193). Instead, for Farrell universal pragmatics goes awry when, contrary to the Austin-Searle tradition of language pragmatics, Habermas dichotomizes speech acts into two domains: the strategic-perlocutionary and the rational-illocutionary. As Allen W. Wood, whom Farrell cites, points out: "Habermas wants to identify the distinction between perlocutionary and illocutionary acts with the distinction he draws between 'orientation to success and orientation to understanding' (*Erfolgs-und-Verständigungs-orientierung*). He wants to understand this not as a distinction between two ways of looking at the same action, but as two different and mutually exclusive ways of acting" (158). That is to say, whereas for Austin and Searle the locutionary, illocutionary, and perlocutionary are assumed to be operative within any given speech act, for Habermas the illocutionary and perlocutionary are disjoined "both categorically and hierarchically" (Farrell 193). This dichotomization or bifurcation of speech acts by Habermas is crucial for Farrell since it schematically devalues the art of rhetoric or practical speech, robs it of any rational and ethical significance, and disallows the possibility of "productive placement for the creative arts of reason, including those of rhetoric" (198). That is to say, insofar as rhetoric is a form of discursive action that, in its suspension of the truthfulness or sincerity claim, must be relegated to the nonreflective domain of strategy, it can make no contribution whatsoever to our collective movement toward mutual understanding. As Farrell states:

It is not simply that, according to certain idealized speech situation criteria, rhetorical speech is flawed and distorted. It is that rhetorical speech is assumed to be mainly strategic speech, oriented toward success. . . . [W]ithin universal pragmatics, rhetoric constitutes a crude subset of *perlocutionary speech*. For Habermas, this means that it is denied any of the reflective validity claims that he presupposes for the *illocutionary* realm known as communicative action.

Extending the implications of this position a bit further may explain why rhetoric could be dismissed as immature. For if we accept Habermas's rather rarefied conception of argumentation as the prototype for a reason-based philosophy of communicative action, and if we accept the relegation of rhetoric to the nonreflective domain of strategy, then rhetoric could be seen as a flawed, transitory stage in the maturation of human nature—hardly the sort of thing to write a book about. (194)

Of course Farrell is writing a book about rhetoric and, more specifically, a book about the centrality of the art of public speech for postmodernity. Rather than turn away from universal pragmatics altogether in order to do so, however, Farrell sets himself to the task of expanding the illocutionary domain so as to make it possible for a Habermasian conception of communicative reason to include rhetoric as a practice that, as Farrell puts it on the very first page of his book, is best understood as "the collaborative art of addressing and guiding decision and judgment" (1) without "damaging the core normative perspective of [Habermas's] project" (202–3). In this effort, Farrell invokes the work of Chaim Perelman and Kenneth Burke, the former for his theorization of audience receptivity as a "normatively significant condition" (203–4) and the latter for his theorization of the way in which "the normative pervades all symbolic action" (208). By putting Habermas into conversation with Perelman and Burke, then, Farrell aims to articulate a revised version of universal pragmatics in which, to borrow the words of José Ortega y Gasset, "[pure] reason . . . surrender[s] its authority to vital reason" (59).

I believe Farrell is right to interrogate Habermas's distinction between the illocutionary and perlocutionary, between speech acts that are oriented to success and speech acts that are oriented to understanding. I also believe, however, that neither Farrell's scrutinization of that dichotomy nor his renovation of universal pragmatics goes far enough. As I have already noted, Farrell's project overall attempts to broaden the scope of the illocutionary so as to make a place for rhetoric within it. In other words, he does not challenge the viability of the distinction between the illocutionary and perlocutionary per se that shores up Habermas's universal pragmatics and that is absolutely necessary to his being able to posit the constative speech act as central, but instead presses the claim that if Habermas were to adopt a less reified conception of argumentative speech he would be obliged to resituate the art of rhetoric under the heading of the illocutionary and, thus, recognize its contribution to the manufacturing of a vital "we." In the final analysis, Farrell's friendly emendations to universal pragmatics respect rather than challenge Habermas's pivotal assumption that communicative understanding is at once the immanent arche and telos of every act of speaking, an assumption that, as the remaining pages of this chapter will show, Kenneth Burke's work renders not merely suspect but thoroughly nonviable and, even more to the point, inimical to a retheorization of the relation of subject and structure and, hence, of social change that discerns in the symbolic or discursive practices of the present the opening for a future that is something other than a repetition or projection of the self-same.

The Limits of Two Theories, or the Productive Possibilities of Failure

At the beginning of this chapter I claimed that Habermas's universal pragmatics is one of the most promising of all recent attempts to construct a theory of social relations and human emancipation for postmodernity. This is not a claim from which I now aim to retreat, for I do believe that Habermas has taken great strides toward articulating a theory of collective life that, as I put it before, aims to be at once antiessentialist, mindful of history, cognizant of the complexities that constitute the postmodern predicament, and protective of human agency. Indeed, in my view at least, Habermas's decisive move, and one for which he receives too little credit and for which he has sometimes been taken brutally to task by the left, is his insistence that "since speech is the distinctive and pervasive medium of life at the human level, the theory of communication is the foundational study of the human sciences: it discloses the universal infrastructure of socio-cultural life" (McCarthy 64). Nonetheless, I also want to claim that if we move into Burke's work with an attitude of production rather than protection, we can discern in it the resources necessary to a postmetaphysical theory of the social that, like that of Habermas, understands our being with others as not merely modified by but as perpetually constituted and potentially reconstituted in discursive practice. Importantly, Burke's work neither posits a universalism that disavows differences that matter nor requires a counterfactual realm of self-transparency and idealized discourse in order, as Farrell puts it, "to avoid the problems of infinite regress and relativism" (192) that seem to be part and parcel of the move from subjectivity to positionality. Without wholly preempting the analysis to follow, I will state here that if taken to the end of the line, Burke's theory of rhetoric allows for a thoroughly post-Kantian intersubjective theory of sociality that, like Habermas's, recognizes the intractable need for some immanent ideal. As Burke would put it, a resolutely "realistic" principle of transcendence is necessary if the possibility for community is to be kept alive in these difficult days of rampant difference and division, but it must be one that takes delight in "the subversive world of the partisan struggle" (Martin 120) rather than gains solace from the promise of its ultimate supersession.

In the three preceding chapters I argued that we can read Burke's *A Grammar of Motives*, *A Rhetoric of Motives*, and *The Rhetoric of Religion: Studies in Logology* as a sustained ontological inquiry. The *Grammar*, I argued, answers the question, What is man? by positing a being that is never proper to itself but, instead, is always already an effect of an ongoing or persistent engagement between two resident and irreducible loci of motives, the action locus of motives and the motion locus of motives. The dialectical play of these two loci of motives, which ontologically anchors Burke's thoroughly nonessentialist theory of subjectivity, is, I claimed, newly determined in *A Rhetoric of Motives* as the condition of possibility for sociality and individuation, for identification and difference, that obliges us to acknowledge the provisional and catachrestical character of any particular social formation or set of social relations whose mode of existence is rhetorical. Finally, I asserted that *The Rhetoric of Religion* can be read as Burke's attempt to account for the movement of the dialectic that is both the precondition and correlate of being human and our being together. His theory of the negative, I suggested, is the resource or capacity "inborn in man" that inaugurates and animates all human life and human history. At this point, then, it would not be a stretch to characterize the previous three chapters as my own attempt to temporalize the essential in Burkeian dramatism and logology, to chart the uneven emergence of Burke's now famous definition of man:

> Man is
> the symbol-using (symbol-making, symbol-misusing) animal
> inventor of the negative (or moralized by the negative)
> separated from his natural condition by instruments of his own
>   making
> goaded by the spirit of hierarchy (or moved by the sense of order)
> and rotten with perfection. (1966a, 16)

Of all but the last line I have already written to a greater or lesser degree. Before turning my attention to it, however, I want to return to or turn back upon the negative, the principle of principles in Burke's work that admonishes us to rebuke the temporal priority of the Habermasian conception of communicative understanding and, thus, to move toward an alternative theorization of the dynamic relations of subject and structure.

In the years intervening between the publication of *A Rhetoric of Motives* and *The Rhetoric of Religion*, Burke wrote an essay entitled "A Dramatistic View of the Origins of Language." Originally printed in *The Quarterly Journal of Speech* and later collected in the volume of essays called *Language as Symbolic Action: Essays on Life, Literature, and Method*, this piece explicitly focuses on Burke's principle of the negative that, as I argued in chapter four, would resurface in *The Rhetoric of Religion* as the originary but never positively present "ground" of the dialectic and, thus, of "our common life together." "This chapter," Burke writes, "is a kind of *tour de force*, locating the specific nature of language in the ability to use the Negative" (1966b, 419). Inaugurating the work with a sentence whose wry humor cuts two ways at once, that both announces and ironically undermines the importance of the essay (since ultimately the piece will celebrate the rhetorical ingenuity of even the most mundane or infantile of utterances), Burke makes clear in the introduction that his goal is to carefully delineate a definition of the negative that, by virtue of its taking "the thought of the negative command" as its necessary starting point, is decidedly different from all other accounts of it, whether formalist, scientist, or anthropologically pragmatist. He writes:

There are many notable aspects of language, such as classification, specification, abstraction, which have their analogues in purely nonverbal behavior. But the negative is a peculiarly linguistic resource. And because it is so peculiarly linguistic, the study of man as the specifically word-using animal requires special attention to this distinctive marvel, the negative.

Consider the *via negationis* in theology; or those related projects in which "non-being" is taken as the ground of being (cf. Boehme's *Ungrund*, or even Kant's dialectic whereby, having summed up the positive world as the "conditioned," he grounds this in the idea of God as the "unconditioned"); or Spinoza's strategic definition in his *Ethics*, "all determination is negation"; or Hegel's principle of Negativity, proclaimed in his *Phenomenology of Mind* as the character of existence; or the adaptation of this in the Marxist dialectic. (1966b, 419–20)

With a gesture that is as bold as it is brief, Burke at once underscores the ubiquitous character of the negative and indicts a whole philosophical tradition for having reified it, charging all these philosophers with having fallen victim to a naive verbal realism that, by discounting the "linguistic factor," ultimately leads them to mistakenly presume that the imperative is to be derived from the indicative, that the prescriptive finds its footing in and gains its bearings from the descriptive, that, as Habermas will later submit, the possibility of "the good and true life" is to be predicated upon the intersubjective vindication of truth claims or constative speech acts. Whereas this entire lot of philosophers tackles the negative from a more or less explicitly scientistic perspective, Burke broaches the issue from a dramatistic point of view. By juxtaposing his own take on the negative to Bergson's approach to it—a less than clear-cut case whose scientistic commitments but delightfully subtle dramatistic leanings make it the perfect test case—Burke is able to summarily state with considerable clarity and precision what is meticulously elaborated in the subsequent fifty-plus pages. He writes:

By a "Dramatistic" approach to the negative, as contrasted with the somewhat "Scientist" emphasis in Bergson, we mean: Whereas Bergson starts from problems of truth or falsity, we start from problems of action. Each approach obviously involves the other. And the situation is further complicated by the fact that Bergson's point about the importance of *expectation* in the functioning of the negative is, in our terms, quite "Dramatistic."

Bergson approaches the problem of the negative in terms of the negative *proposition*; but we would approach it in terms of the negative *command*. Where he would build his analysis of the negative about a sentence in the indicative mood, such as "The thing is not here," we would build ours about a sentence in the imperative, such as "Do not do that." We would say that the negative must have begun as a rhetorical or hortatory function, *as with the negatives of the Ten Commandments*. (1966b, 421)

If we could be absolutely certain that the paradigmatic expression or perfect realization of a principle carries within itself the necessary conditions for its emergence *writ small*, that is to say, if we could be sure that a thoroughly continuous relation obtains between origins and ends, then by this point in the essay Burke would have already made the case that the very essence of language can be derived from the hortatory negative. "Unfortunately, however," as he notes, "as soon as we decide on such Codification of Conscience for our model of the Perfect Negative, we find another shift necessary"; namely, "we must ask whether the negative need originally have been such at all" (1966b, 422). Thus in the following three sections of the essay Burke turns his attention to answering this question and presents a genealogy of the negative that specifies three successive stages. Without discounting the "pre-language of sensation and gesture" that may be conceived as "a purely behavioristic negative," Burke nevertheless argues that the matrix or ground for the emergence of the hortatory or admonitory "no" is to be located in what he calls "the prehistorical beginning of language," that moment in which, as he describes it:

[T]he primal ancestor would be closer to a verb than to any other part of speech. At least it would be verbal in the sense that it had strongly *imperative* or *hortatory* connotations, and grammarians usually grant such functions only to verbal modes. Such a "pre-negative" verb could have been a mere tonal gesture for calling-attention-to. It would have been less like a negative than like the gruntlike sounds an incipiently vocal infant makes when handing something to an adult, or when asking something of an adult, or when noticing something in which it takes an interest. (1966b, 423)

Significantly enough, the "no" at this particular time "while *implying* a negative . . . would still not be felt as an out-and-out negative command" (1966b, 424) but would, instead, seem "as positive as any word like *run*, or *eat*, or *fight*, and the like, except that it had a hortatory nature which such words do not primarily possess" (1966b, 424). Following this prehistorical phase of the implied negative in connotations of deterrence is a series of intermediate stages "during which the admonitory word came to function *like an auxiliary verb in the imperative*" (1966b, 424). In other words, at this time "an expression like *man no run* would be literally translatable not as 'the man does not run' or even as 'the man should not run,' but as 'man beware run' or 'man caution run'. A little further along would be: 'man stop run' " (1966b, 424). It is during this stage that we witness the emergence of the attitudinal negative or the adaptation of the negative to ideas of fear and doubt as well as the transition to the explicit negative of command. The third and final stage to which Burke turns his attention is distinguished by the advent of the "out-and-out propositional negative." About it he writes:

[T]erms for doubt would probably be the point at which the out-and-out propositional negative emerged. We mean that from this point on, the negative *qua* negative would be felt in a given linguistic system. It would have come of age, no longer being felt merely as a modification of admonitory verbs, but as the kind of particle used in the purely *indicative* distinction between "it is" and "it is not."

In brief, when you get to *doubt*, you're within the *scientist* area of *information*. So your next step is the outright *No* of "negative propositions" that affirm a "negative fact." (1966b, 425)

What Burke's "journey from the command negative, through the attitudinal negative, to the out-and-out propositional negative" (1966b, 459) seeks to establish and what the remaining pages of the essay aim to confirm is that "the very essence of language" and, hence, all utterances from the most simple to the most complex are correctly derived "from the ability to use the negative as negative" (1966b, 422).

It is hardly necessary to explicate further Burke's analysis of the "Idea of No" that is so central to the dramatistic perspective in order to discern in it the opening for a thoroughgoing critique of Habermas's universal pragmatics. To put it all too boldly perhaps, what a Burkeian or dramatistic account on the origins of language undermines is the primacy of communicative understanding with the possibility for a consensus that is embedded within it. "What raises us out of nature," Habermas writes, "is the only thing whose nature we can know: *language*. Through its structure, autonomy and responsibility are posited for us. Our first sentence expresses unequivocally the intention of universal and unconstrained consensus" (McCarthy 287). What I am arguing at this point, then, is not simply that Burke's genealogy of the negative enables us to recognize that Habermas advances a too narrow conception of rhetoric (although this is most certainly the case as the prior discussion suggests and the ensuing pages will clearly demonstrate). I am also not merely claiming, as Farrell does, for example, that a Burkeian take on the negative provides the warrant for an expanded conception of the illocutionary domain of language that would then make it possible for universal pragmatics to acknowledge rather than disavow the contributions of rhetoric to collective life. What I am arguing is that Burke's dramatistic account of the origins of language is the first step toward the deconstruction of the illocutionary/perlocutionary binary that grants the communicative both temporal and logical priority and privilege over the rhetorical in universal pragmatics. In other words, the "Idea of No" puts us on the track of the radical critique of universal pragmatics by inverting its resident hierarchy, by repositioning the hortatory gesture or perlocutionary speech act as that which is temporally prior and, hence, holds the superior position. If, as Burke suggests, the very essence of language is to be derived from the principle of the negative or the "Idea of No," which, in contrast to the "Idea of Nothing," serves to "stress its original *persuasiveness*" (1966b, 458), then there is no communicative praxis that is not always and already rhetorical praxis or a derivation thereof.

As I indicated in chapter one in the context of laying out the manner in which I would read Burke's trivium of motives and as I have noted elsewhere as well (1992), the deconstruction of texts does not terminate in the overthrow or inversion of a binary, however violent. This reversal must be displaced, the term now holding the superior position must be put under erasure so as to make room for, as Derrida puts it, "the irruptive emergence of a new 'concept,' a concept which no longer allows itself to be understood in terms of the previous regime" (1976, lxxvii) or prior established system of oppositions. In order to work such a displacement it is necessary to do a bit of backtracking, to recall the pivotal assumptions and crucial logical maneuvers that traffic under the name *universal pragmatics*. Hence, although I have written it more than once before, I will repeat it here: first, in Habermas's view communicative understanding is immanent in all utterance; its purest mode of actualization, however, is the constative speech act whose condition of emergence on a general or grand scale is the ideal speech situation. Second, it is not at all fortuitous that the constative speech act belongs to a language domain that is strictly differentiated from the language domain within which both rhetorical and literary or poetic discourses are said to belong or to operate. While on the one hand the constative speech act is an exemplar of nonstrategic illocutionary speech or speech oriented toward understanding, on the other hand rhetorical and literary discourses are classified as instances of strategic perlocutionary speech or speech oriented toward success. Third, and for reasons that have already been discussed, illocutionary speech acts are not, in Habermas's view, simply other than perlocutionary speech acts. To paraphrase Burke, the difference between *this* speech act and *that* speech act always entails a difference between *this kind of* speech act and *that kind of* speech act, which is to say it always entails the issue of value or class (understood in a logological rather than economic sense). Furthermore, for Habermas the valuative difference between illocutionary and perlocutionary speech acts is, most significantly, that the promise of the productive transformation of social relations resides in the former and is hopelessly deferred by the latter.

It is important here to point out that in claiming as I did above that Burke's genealogy of the negative not only contests but also overturns what Habermas takes to be the priority and privilege of communicative praxis, I did not challenge the viability of the way in which he defines the one term over and against the other. That is to say, so far all I have done is to claim that Burke's essay on the origins of language inverts Habermas's resident hierarchy and repositions the rhetorical or discourse that is persuasive and success oriented as the controlling term. However, what about this distinction between the illocutionary and the perlocutionary or the communicative and the rhetorical that corresponds to the spacing between the nonstrategic and the strategic, between utterances oriented to understanding and those oriented to success? Of course, I am neither the first reader of Habermas's work to question this binary or cast a suspicious glance upon it nor the first to respond to it, and the response, as one would reasonably expect given that we stand in the twilight of subjectivity, usually charges Habermas with having founded his entire project on an altogether theoretically and practically bankrupt Enlightenment notion: intentionality. As Bill Martin, whose stance is representative of that of critics whose engagement with poststructuralism incites them to move into the Habermasian edifice with considerable caution,[2] argues:

[Habermas's] conception certainly has its merits. The problem is whether it really is grounded in something other than a reworked subject-centered reason. The key notion that we have been circling around for these last several pages is *intention.* Habermas's move from Chomsky to Searle and speech act theory was motivated, from the start and throughout, by a need for intention as pragmatic ground. It is clear that the supposedly non-social realm of strategic action is governed by the intentions of agents. Habermas does not care to deny this. The notion of "lifeworld," however, which Habermas takes from Husserl, also has intentionality at its center, as does Searle's speech act theory. . . . Even a certain spreading out of the rational will, if it is still grounded in intentionality, remains a philosophy of the subject. (93)

One of the lessons Martin takes from Derrida and finds in Donald Davidson's work as well is that language will never thoroughly abide by our intentions; that we are as much written by a language as we are writers of it; that in the midst of our intending in language, something other is always already taking place. By carefully retracing the case that Derrida makes in regard to "the understanding of language as 'literary' "—and by this, Martin correctly states, Derrida means "that 'literature' is that part of language that foregrounds the differential workings of language and that there is no part of language that is finally free of this 'literary' quality" (108)—Martin shows that the categorical or pragmatic distinction on which Habermas insists between the illocutionary and the perlocutionary simply does not hold. As Martin puts it, "language will not submit itself, even under threat of force, to being defined as essentially communicative" (104).

To be sure, Martin's interrogation of Habermas's reliance upon intentionality, however veiled, causes the line between the illocutionary and the perlocutionary to begin to waver and, thus, universal pragmatics to begin to tremble. But the critique that wrenches open a vista through which we can see in language's recalcitrant and exorbitant relationship to intention "new possibilities . . . for the ways that we live in the world" (107) also has its limits, one of which Martin himself duly notes: "And yet, if Habermas's pragmatic program is read in a less tendentious light, perhaps we need only admit that intentions count for something, and that, if we are ever going to turn this world in the direction of greater social justice, we have to be able to depend on something basic in social interactions that always already intends this transformation" (95). However, a second limitation of the critique of the illocutionary/perlocutionary binary that centers itself on the problematics of intentionality is that while the critique threatens universal pragmatics by emphasizing that the irruptive possibilities of "writing in its general sense" cannot be thoroughly bracketed out or that the "literary" cannot be altogether purged even when we think of speech in Habermas's restricted sense as communicative, it does not directly address that other "crude subset of *perlocutionary speech*" (Farrell 194): rhetoric. Obviously, rhetoric or persuasive discourse that, as Habermas conceives it, is "oriented to success" would, like any other articulation, also always be vulnerable to the poststructuralist critique of intentionality, but Habermas could quite conceivably concede this point and still affirm the viability of the illocutionary/perlocutionary binary. He could, so to speak, play fast and loose with the term "oriented," make it a case of "more or less," and assert the following: while illocutionary speech acts (whose paradigmatic example is the constative utterance or truth claim) are "oriented" toward understanding, perlocutionary

speech acts (whose paradigmatic example is rhetoric taken as persuasion and not as mere figuration) are "oriented" toward success.[3]

What about this concept of "success," however, that makes it
possible for Habermas to classify rhetoric as a subset of perlocutionary speech? Is Habermas justified in claiming that a categorical distinction can be made between rhetorical and communicative practices on the grounds that the former are success oriented whereas
the latter are not? About this distinction Habermas writes, "It seems
to me that *strategic action* ('oriented to the actor's success'—in general, modes of action that correspond to the utilitarian model of
purposive-rational action) as well as (the still-insufficiently-analyzed)
symbolic action (e.g., a concert, a dance—in general, modes of action
that are bound to non-propositional systems of symbolic expression)
differ from communicative action in that individual validity claims
are suspended (in strategic action, truthfulness, in symbolic action,
truth)" (1979b, 41). I do not want to challenge—nor would Burke—
the claim that sometimes, perhaps even all too often, rhetoricians
withhold their intentions in the attempt to ensure a particular aim or
effect. Indeed, the history of public oratory is in large part a record of
such attempts, the more malign of which constitute our checkered
past. However, as I noted above, this is not Habermas's claim; he is
making a categorical distinction, positing a definition of rhetoric
that portends universal applicability, not recounting what Todorov
has acutely termed "[t]he [s]plendor and [m]isery of [r]hetoric" (60)
over time. And it is precisely this claim, this definition of rhetoric,
that Burke's work helps us to put under erasure.

From beginning to end, Burke's work resists the near habitual tendency on the part of philosophers and theorists of language to reduce
rhetoric or "the competitive use of the cooperative" to speech acts
oriented toward success. Although his explicit and fully elaborated
case against this perspective is presented in the final and quite remarkable section of *A Rhetoric of Motives* entitled "Pure Persuasion," the groundwork for it is already being prepared in the closing
pages of the *Grammar*. There Burke writes, "The Rhetoric, which
would study the 'competitive use of the cooperative,' would be designed to help us take delight in the Human Barnyard, with its addic-
tion to the Scramble, an area that would cause us great unhappiness
could we not transcend it by appreciation, classifying and tracing
back to their beginnings in Edenic simplicity those linguistic modes
of suasion that often seem little better than malice and the lie" (1962,
442). In emphasizing the pleasure that can come from an inquiry into
the "competitive use of the cooperative," Burke is not denying that
even the most "perfect" of those strategic speech acts that suspend
the truthfulness or sincerity claim—"the lie"—falls within the scope

of the study of rhetoric. What he is denying, however, is that an adequate definition of rhetoric can be derived by analyzing only the more superficial features or manifest aspects of such speech acts. Indeed, to regard rhetoric primarily as a means to success, to see it as only the use of symbols in the "quest for advantage," is not only to efface the considerable complexity of any rhetorical event, but also to discount the enjoyable aspect of rhetorical action per se. On the latter of these two points Burke writes in the culminating section of *A Rhetoric of Motives*:

[T]hough what we mean by pure persuasion in the absolute sense exists nowhere, it can be present as a motivational ingredient in any rhetoric, no matter how intensely advantage-seeking such rhetoric may be. . . .
   Pure persuasion involves the saying of something, not for an extra-verbal advantage to be got by the saying, but because of a satisfaction intrinsic to the saying. It summons because it likes the feel of a summons. It would be nonplused if the summons were answered. It attacks because it revels in the sheer syllables of vituperation. It would be horrified if, each time it finds a way of saying, "Be damned," it really did send a soul to rot in hell. It intuitively says, "This is so," purely and simply because this is so. (1962, 793)

No doubt, in taking the pleasure that is effected by "the process of appeal for itself alone, without ulterior purpose" (1962, 522) into account, Burke has already moved well beyond the scope of Habermas's definition of rhetoric. That is to say, by seeing in the process of appeal an "otherworldly" aspect, by attending to a facet of appeal that is wildly exorbitant to its "use value" in a pragmatic sense, Burke exposes the limits of thinking of rhetoric exclusively in terms of, to use Habermas's words, "its prosaic, innerworldly functions" (1987, 205). Rhetoric cannot, indeed will not, be so contained. But there is more.

   In the third and last part of *A Rhetoric of Motives* to which I have already referred, Burke explicitly and without reserve presents a definition of rhetoric that is diametrically opposed to Habermas's. In Burke's view, rhetorical or persuasive speech acts are most certainly not oriented toward success for the simple, albeit on first glance perversely counterintuitive, reason that "a persuasion that succeeds, dies" (1962, 798). While it is certainly true that rhetorical or suasory speech taken in the narrow sense often hits its mark and moves an audience to a particular action or incites in them a particular attitude, the rhetorical or suasory in the general sense is neither engendered nor sustained by a restricted and pragmatic economy of means-end or need-satisfaction but, to the contrary, is animated by a desire that in principle is insatiable. "To go on eternally (as form does)," Burke tells us, "[persuasion] could not be directed merely towards attainable advantages" (1962, 798). In fact, at the precise moment a discourse encroaches upon or seizes the object(ive) that would be its end, another is ushered in to take its place. As Burke points out, even the seemingly banal and "frenzied human cult of advantage, the quest of many things that cannot bring real advantage yet are obtainable, would likewise seem ultimately to require such a 'meta-rhetorical' explanation. (At least, this would account for its *origins*. Institutional factors would account for its *intensity*)" (1962, 798). He writes:

Insofar as a society rejects interference "from within" as a device for per-petuating the persuasive act, men can still get the same result by a cult of "new needs" (with the continual shifting of objectives to which men are goaded by the nature of our economic system). By such temporizings, the form of persuasion is permanently maintained. For in proportion as men, threatened with the loss of persuasion through attaining its object, turn to court other objects, such constant shifting of purposes in effect supplies (as it seems, "from without") the principle of self-interference which the per-petuating of the persuasive act demands. To make the attaining of A but the condition for the need of B, and the attaining of B but the condition of the need of C, etc., adds up to the same "form" as if one merely went on forever courting A at a distance. A single need, forever courted, as on Keats's Grecian Urn, would be made possible by self-interference. Drop self-interference, plunge "extravertedly" into the "rat race" of new needs forever changing, and you get the equivalent. (1962, 798–99)

But Burke's definition of rhetoric that understands suasory discourse as operated by a structure of desire whose object(ive) is always al-ready unobtainable, always already deferred, does not explain only the more mundane or, better yet, profane of appeals; it also makes it possible for us to account for those that are most sacred:

Biologically, it is of the essence of man to desire. But by the same token, biologically it is of the essence of man to be sated. Only the motives of "mys-tery" (making for development towards ever "higher" degrees of ordination) are infinite in their range, as a child learns for himself when he first thinks of counting "to the highest number."
The dialectical transcending of reality through symbols is at the roots of this mystery, at least so far as naturalistic motives are concerned. It culmi-nates in pure persuasion, absolute communication, beseechment for itself alone, praise and blame so universalized as to have no assignable physical object (hence it is led to postulate the Principles of Goodness and Evil in general, as the only "audience" possible for an address so generalized). (1962, 799)

Burke is careful to note that he is "not discovering 'God' here, in the theologian's sense" but, instead, coming upon it by moving strictly along "the verbal route" (1962, 800–801). Whereas for the theologian God "must be much more than an 'Idea' dialectically arrived at," for the dramatist whose task it is to come to terms with symbolic acts, God is quite a different matter. All in all, Burke writes, "our point is":

Here, in this conclusion of dialectic, one should look for the ultimate rhetorical motive of *homo dialecticus*. Human effort would thus be grounded not in the search for "advantage," and in the mere "sublimating" of that search by "rationalizations" and "moralizations." Rather, it would be grounded in a *form*, in the persuasiveness of the hierarchic order itself. And considered dialectically, prayer, as pure beseechment, would be addressed not to an *object*, (which might "answer" the prayer by providing booty) but to the *hierarchic principle itself*, where the answer is implicit in the address. (1962, 800)

For Burke, then, rhetorical speech is speech that has no goal proper, no proper object(ive), no particular for. "Rhetoric," as Burke put it approximately a hundred pages earlier in the book, "is thus made from fragments of dialectic" (1962, 699) that if needs be will, in Kierkegardian fashion, "transform courtship into prayer" (1962, 776) so as to "court . . . in terms of eternity, that is, in perpetual repetition" (1962, 774)—and to do so outside the economy of specific gain, always already at a requisite distance from the possibility of success, completion, consumption, unification.

  It is precisely this definition of rhetoric—rhetoric understood as a mode of discourse whose continued "existence" is predicated upon its own perpetual failure or its irreducible inability to achieve its end—that Burke claims underwrites all communicative exchange, all symbolic action. He states, " '[P]ure persuasion' is an absolute, logically prior to any one persuasive act" (1962, 776); not only is it "the essence of language," it is also the essence of communication: "In its essence communication involves the use of verbal symbols for purposes of appeal. Thus, it splits formally into the three elements of speaker, speech, and spoken-to, with the speaker so shaping his speech as to 'commune with' the spoken-to" (1962, 795). In the final analysis, then, while Burke's genealogy on the negative runs directly counter to Habermas's claim that communicative understanding is temporally prior to the rhetorical or hortatory use of symbols, Burke's thinking on the essential character and structure of persuasion or rhetoric *as such* questions radically the logical priority of communicative understanding as well. To cite once again a famous passage from the *Rhetoric* that becomes ever more salient in the context of this discussion: "If men were not apart from one another, there would be no need for the rhetorician to proclaim their unity. If men were wholly and truly of one substance, absolute communication would be of man's very essence. It would not be an ideal, as it now is, partly embodied in material conditions and partly frustrated by these same conditions; rather it would be as natural, spontaneous, and total as with those ideal prototypes of communication, the theologian's angels, or 'messengers' " (1962, 546). As the above citation indicates, however, the point is not to privilege rhetoric in the narrow sense over understanding in the Habermasian sense, but to recognize that the latter, as much as the former, is underwritten by an ineluctable economy of difference that simply cannot be overcome.

Not only is it the case that the economy of difference that is the condition of possibility for any symbolic action cannot be superseded; according to Burke, we also would be mistaken to even wish it otherwise, for in a dramatistic view, it is precisely the lack of complete understanding that keeps the desire for community alive. According to Burke, it is precisely because all human relations are vexed by the paradox of substance rather than underwritten by the logic of identity that any coupling, any community, is always already a project in the making, always already, as I stated in the opening pages of this chapter, an evocation rather than a yet to be actualized condition or foregone conclusion. For Burke, that is to say, it is precisely the impossibility of closing the gap between self and other that keeps us engaged with one another, talking to one another, courting one another; that forever keeps us "promot[ing] social cohesion by acting rhetorically upon [our]selves and one another" (1962, 522). Indeed, as Burke has put it so simply and elegantly, "[i]dentification is affirmed with earnestness precisely because there is division. Identification is compensatory to division" (1962, 546). Thus, paradoxical as it may be, our very being-with is predicated upon our always already being other: a vital *sensus communis* is sustained by resolute difference and division or, to put it a bit differently, a vivacious "we" exists only insofar as its total realization is an ever-receding possibility, only insofar as its actualization is a to-come. Finally, then, Burke's work not only leads us to interrogate the viability of positing communicative understanding as the beginning point for a theory of the social but, moreover, invites us to question the wisdom of positioning or fashioning "consensus" as an ideal.

But one matter remains: if we are to admit that communicative understanding is a ruse and consensus a dead end, on what are we to pin our hopes for a future that will be something other than more of the same? While the very *formulation* of the question implies that we need to move well beyond universal pragmatics, *formulating* an answer to it necessitates a movement beyond Burkeian dramatism and logology as well in the sense that the condition of possibility for its articulation depends upon our deploying precisely that which has been "repressed" or, as Burke would put it, "discounted" by his own texts: the full force of the negative.

Among other things, what I hope this study has done is to make a strong case for the centrality of the principle of the negative in Burke's thinking. The "Idea of No" over and against the "Idea of Nothing," I have argued, is the ontologically secured but resolutely rhetorical, and, hence, irreducibly intersubjective, condition of possibility for transcending social estrangement, which does not, however, gain its force from a transcendental guarantee that is either anterior to, posterior to, or inscribed within it. That is to say, although the principle of the negative "is that capacity inborn to man" that inaugurates the movement of the dialectic and, thus, the historical emergence—or, better yet, rhetorical invention—of selves and societies, it does not determine the particular constitution, character, or disposition of those selves or those societies. To say this much, however, is already to step a certain critical distance beyond dramatism and logology proper, to usher back in to the Burkeian enclosure all that it methodologically sought to expel so as to offer its own rounded account of human motivation that could justifiably "lay claim to a universal validity" (1962, xix)—namely, temporality understood as radical undecidability, potential discontinuity, and rupture and, thus, as a resource of social change. If, then, we wrestle back into dramatism and logology that which they imperfectly exclude so as to pry them open anew, it becomes possible for us to notice that temporality (a "structure" that cannot be contained by structurality) is the irreducible and always imperfectly excluded force that, in relentlessly applying pressure upon the movement of the dialectic from within, keeps it forever open to the possibility of failure. That is to say, temporality is that which ensures that the dialectic arising out of the principle of the negative always already carries within it the structural possibility of the failed sublation and is that which secures the chance that the negation of the negation will misfire, that the sublation, understood in the Hegelian sense as a unified supersession, will not be produced. Taken as a constituent component of a dialectic now thought of in its broadest sense, that is to say, as not a priori clamped closed, temporality is the haphazard and unruly force that constitutes a spatiotemporal breach that makes possible a human intervention that may interrupt or divert what appears to be destined. I would even go so far as to suggest that this notion of the open or asymmetrical dialectic is the unwitting gift of the appendix to *The Rhetoric of Religion* entitled "Epilogue: Prologue in Heaven," a text that at this point we could most certainly read as a satirical performance of Habermas's ideal speech situation. There Burke writes: "But once the successiveness of time (and its similarly divisible partner, space) introduces the possibility of an interval between the command and the obedience, by the same token there is the possibility of disobedience"

(1970, 278). What Burke intimates in this single sentence is that situated within the "interval" is the possibility for a future that is not simply a future-present, but a radically other future whose conditions of realization are given over to us as a promise but whose actualization rests solely upon us. To be sure, such actualization will, as Burke has put it, "all center in [our] way of using the negative" (1970, 278), in our willingness to rhetorically transform ourselves in the mirror of politics by *actively choosing* to become its new subjects. And that, as I stated in the first chapter of this book, is the responsibility, the risk, indeed the burden of anyone whose most precious and precocious wish is to enter into the fray we have always called history and we now call postmodernity.

Notes

1. Entering the Fray

1. Ernesto Laclau's recent essay entitled "Community and Its Paradoxes: Richard Rorty's 'Liberal Utopia' " is a notable exception. In this essay Laclau explicitly invokes the term *persuasion*. However, what at first appears to be a strong sense of persuasion ultimately gives way to the theory of articulation that reduces rhetoric to the irruptive possibilities entailed in the figural excesses of language, a theory whose limits are addressed in the discussion that follows.

2. See, for example, the works of Cary Nelson, Trevor Melia, and David Williams.

3. It is interesting to notice that nearly every investigation into Burke's work is initiated by the discovery of a seemingly irresolvable contradiction within one of Burke's works that, minimally, threatens to dismantle the integrity of the particular work under analysis or, even worse, harbors the capacity to radically compromise the unity and coherence of the entire Burke corpus. For example, in his article "Kenneth Burke on Form," Robert Heath locates in *A Grammar of Motives* "a shift from a predominantly psychological orientation" to one that "emphasizes attributes inherent in language" (393). Working well within a hermeneutic that presupposes a unity of meaning, Heath is obliged to treat the break in Burke's thought as ultimately intelligible in terms of a univocal totality whose semantic value derives from the internal relation of the parts to one another. Similarly, for William Rueckert an adequate interpretation of Burke's work emerges only with the discovery of a cognitive pattern that binds together two seemingly incongruous "movements" in the history of Burke's thought. He writes, "One move-

ment in Burke's curve of development . . . comes to a close in *The Philosophy of Literary Form*, and another begins in *A Grammar of Motives*. The stages in the first are from creative artist to literary critic to social critic to the fusion of literary and social criticism. . . . The second movement begins where the first ends. This time it is from literary and social criticism to the discipline which Burke believes will include all others: the analysis of language and linguistic action—what he has recently called 'Logology' " (1963, 129). In order to accord to Burke's corpus the authority of a complete and coherent totality, Rueckert locates in the texts a belated logic of sublimation—the crisis of discontinuity is managed by way of a larger synthesizing structure that reconciles parts in a whole. Over the course of the history of Burkeian criticism, it is Rene Wellek's interrogation that poses the most serious threat to the hermeneutic appropriation of Burke's work. The Burke corpus resists interpretation, Wellek argues, because it records an entire series of seemingly random theoretical shifts: "The earliest pieces included in *Counter-Statement* (1931) can be described as implying an advocacy of an art for art's sake position, while later essays in the same book indicate a shift to psychological and social criticism. . . . *Permanence and Change* (1935) and *Attitudes Toward History* (1937) represent [his] Marxist stage. In the later 'thirties, in the essays collected as *The Philosophy of Literary Form* (1941), Burke returned to more strictly literary concerns, which he then again subordinated to the elaboration of his general scheme expounded in *A Grammar of Motives* (1945) and *A Rhetoric of Motives* (1950). The new volume, *Language as Symbolic Action* (1966), which collects essays of the 'fifties and 'sixties, constitutes a partial return to literary criticism" (173). With Wellek, the possibility of a resolution of part/whole relations into a unity that is the condition of intelligibility and meaningfulness seems all but foreclosed. Each successive theoretical realignment on Burke's part makes it ever more difficult to conclude that the texts can be assembled into a formal or semantic unity. However, as in the case of Heath and Rueckert, Wellek ultimately overcomes the potentially undermining force of discontinuity and preserves the integrity of the corpus by incorporating the partial and particular significations into a narrative structure whose informing principle derives from the texts themselves.

Though inhabiting at the outset a scene characterized by enigma, mystery, irresoluteness, and doubt, critics of the Burke corpus finish with an explication of the texts that reconfirms both the integrity and self-sufficiency of the text and the strength of a strategy of interpretation that premises self-understanding as the pursuit of universal, which is to say, historically uncontaminated, truths. In Robert Heath's case the rift that vexes Burke's texts is resolved by his rewriting the Burke corpus as a "quest" narrative by means of which, as he puts it, "the essential unity between the two themes can be discovered" (393). Similarly, William Rueckert forges unity out of division by interpreting the corpus as a virtual *Bildungsroman*: the "two movements" in Burke's works are mere stages in the growth of the artist-critic that culminates in an epiphany—"a coherent and total vision, a self-contained and internally consistent way of viewing man, the various scenes in which he lives, and the drama of human relations enacted upon those scenes" (1963,

129). In Rene Wellek's view, the Burke corpus coheres if we diagnose it as the symptomatic expression of a "would be philosopher" suffering from an ultimately debilitating case of the anxiety of multiple influences. Even Fredric Jameson (1982) and Frank Lentricchia (1983), two critics well known for their theoretical attachments to Marxism, produce interpretations of Burke's work from within a hermeneutic tradition that, as I noted earlier, homogenizes the disparate elements of the texts into a unified totality or meaning-structure in order to assess its immanent "truth."

4. For the analysis here I draw heavily upon Jacques Derrida's illuminating essay on the "dangerous supplement" in the texts of Rousseau (1976, 97–164).

2. Reading Ontology in A *Grammar of Motives*

1. It is important to note that in an earlier essay Booth reiterates Burke's caution against an overly reductive approach to human action. He writes, "It would be an equally misleading reduction, possibly even more dangerous, to move in the opposite direction and pretend that man is not in any sense undergoing mere motion. What we offer is a language that can cover both truths, able to move dialectically to encompass the precritical facts of both our animality and our symbolicity" (1974–75, 19–20). William Rueckert also qualifies his earlier interpretation of Burke's action/motion dichotomy as a formidable binary by stating that "[i]t would be a mistake to assume that Burke thinks that man is nothing but an aggregate of symbol-systems. *Man is a symbol-using animal*, in Burke's definition, and the animal part is as important as the symbol-using part" (1982, 9). However, Rueckert neither discusses this thematic at any length nor specifies its implications for Burke's theory of dramatism.

2. For additional readings of the action/motion dichotomy as the distinction that uniquely identifies Burke's ontological presuppositions see Walter Fisher and Wayne Brockriede, Louis Gallo, and Howard Nemerov. Michael Feehan's 1985 essay "Oscillation as Assimilation: Burke's Latest Revisions" confounds the action/motion dichotomy by addressing what has been referred to by Burke as a "metabiological" approach. Feehan's essay does not, however, seek to mark continuities between Burke's later definition of man as "bodies that learn language" and his earlier definition of man as the "symbol-using animal." To the contrary, Feehan argues the later definition marks a deviation from the earlier statement. D. L. Jennerman confounds the action/motion dichotomy by bringing the influence of Freud to it. Jennerman's reading of motion by way of Freud, however, radically textualizes the notion of motion, indeed nearly reconstitutes it as a variant of action.

3. For example, F. P. Dinneen anchors his speculations on *The Rhetoric of Religion* in a reading of the action/motion dichotomy. He writes, "Dramatism assumes 'a qualitative empirical difference between mental action and mechanical motion' which is founded on the 'empirical' distinction between people's behavior toward human beings and things" (178). William Rueckert explicitly states the case in his seminal study *Kenneth Burke and the Drama*

of Human Relations. He writes, "among animals, a sexual or biological urge could be frustrated but not consciously negated; among men, however, such an impulse which, if unchecked, would result in a positive act, can be consciously, willfully negated as well as frustrated. From this phenomenon comes all drama, for the essence of drama is moral choice and willed action" (145). James W. Chesebro makes a similar argument in his recently published essay "Epistemology and Ontology as Dialectical Modes in the Writings of Kenneth Burke." Therein Chesebro writes, "In greater detail, Burke's action-motion dichotomy is critical to this first ontological principle. *Action* specifies the province or realm of the symbolic which provides human beings with their most unique definition, while *motion* specifies the extra symbolic or nonsymbolic operations of nature" (182). This is also the argument Frank Lentricchia makes in his recent book *Criticism and Social Change.* He argues that "[t]he deep bias of his dramatistic system is unavoidably humanistic because the very notion of dramatism rests on the distinction between 'action' (a uniquely human movement) and 'motion' (a process that presumably characterizes all nonhuman movement)" (71). It is interesting to note that Lentricchia reads Burke's earlier book *Permanence and Change* as "the 'fall' into unfreedom" (59), a reading predicated upon the notion that the action differential is not only logically prior to but also temporally prior to the motion differential. See also Bernard L. Brock.

4. This study neither tackles nor aims to cover over the deeply troubling issue of Burke's use of the term *man* and his persistent not noticing of sexual difference. An inquiry into the implications of sexual difference for Burke's theorization of rhetoric will be taken up elsewhere.

5. The strategy for the analysis of motive proposed herein finds its inspiration in Gayatri Spivak's unpublished lectures on Marx delivered at the University of Pittsburgh during the fall term of 1988.

6. My argument here works against Chesebro's claim in his article "Epistemology and Ontology as Dialectical Modes in the Writings of Kenneth Burke" that "[symbol-using] allows human beings to become self-conscious, create motives independently of physical phenomena, and ultimately to create social constructions of reality. In contrast, the world of external phenomena is a world of 'motion,' governed by instinct and intuition, without self-reflection" (182). It is my claim that the action/motion dialectic does not supersede but sublates (in the strict sense of the term) the two constituent elements of being human.

7. Here I am working against even those readings of Burke's action/motion dichotomy that leave room for a human act constituted by either action *or* motion. See, for example, Richard Fiordo's article "Kenneth Burke's Semiotic" wherein he claims both that "[w]ith language, man divides from his animality and joins with his symbolicity" (57) and that "[i]n applying this terministic distinction of Burke's semiotic, it can be seen that an event that occurs and involves a symbol-user may be at the level of motion or action" (66). In counterdistinction to this argument, I am claiming that it is out of the action/motion dichotomy that all human acts are produced; that both differentials are at work in the production of human action.

8. Robert L. Heath's problematization of the action/motion dichotomy does not offer an answer, but does put us on the track of this notion. He writes, "This part of Burke's theory is problematic because he insists that action (including symbolic action) is characterized by will and motion by causality. If the body responds to the mind and the mind to the body in *causal* ways, has he not blurred the distinction he is using as the underpinning of symbolic action?" (1986, 127).

9. Here I distinguish my own reading of the human being or agent in Burke's work from Lentricchia's. By working from the paradox of substance articulated in the *Grammar*, Lentricchia argues that "Burke deconstructs the subject *in order to* historicize it" (1983, 75). While Lentricchia's argument is provocative, I think it is fundamentally misleading, because Burke's notion of substance does not, as a deconstructionist would have it, displace the binary opposition between a thing and its context.

10. In order to make an argument on behalf of Kenneth Burke's "realism" Brock goes so far as to suggest that in his later work "dramatism as a philosophy appears to shift away from 'ambiguity' in favor of 'reality' and resolves the 'action' and 'motion' tension in favor of 'action' " (102). As I will argue in chapter four, this is decidedly not the case. In fact, I will try to show the way in which dialectic as the originary finessing of an action/motion differential that inhabits the human being becomes increasingly more critical in Burke's later work, *The Rhetoric of Religion*.

11. Speaking about Burke's "definition of the human being" Brock writes, "Burke essentially argues that the metaphor, by transcending the contradictions of 'reality,' enables humans to act, and one might also argue that metaphor is one of the human being's 'instruments of his own making' that 'separates man [sic] from his [sic] natural condition' " (97). Here Brock interprets Burke as positing language (i.e., metaphor, tropes) as originary. As I argue, language or verbal action is one determination among many of a more originary finessing. Also, in counterdistinction to my argument, Hugh Dalziel Duncan claims that "motives cannot be explained without reference to their linguistic expression, since motives arise *in* and *through* language. If this is so, we must conceive of language as a basic, not a residual, sociological category" (256). Our difference rests, of course, upon Duncan's key term *sociological*, a term that subtly harbors the ontological presupposition that language, and not the movement of the dialectic itself, is the origin of human being in the world. In his recent book *Kenneth Burke and Martin Heidegger: With a Note Against Deconstruction*, Samuel Southwell argues a similar case: "In Burke's thought, 'act' is the central idea first and last; it is the focus of the structure of becoming which is the culmination of the development of Burke's system, which he usually calls 'Dramatism,' but sometimes 'Logology.' Act is made possible by language, which creates choices, requiring preferences, which are purposes" (30). Like Duncan, Southwell reads language as originary in Burke's system. In chapter three I will explicitly address this issue.

12. Donald A. Stauffer raises this issue by seeing in Burke's justification of the dramatistic method a tautological argument: "[I]f an *act* is needed to

explain a *motive*, we are caught in an unprofitable circle, since one might assume our interest in a motive comes from the belief that it will explain an act. If the Act may be considered 'as Locus of Motives,' why is it considered in their *grammar?*" (184–85).

13. Critics commonly read parts two and three of the *Grammar* as mere applications of the pentad. Even Victor Vitanza, who censures other critics for their reductive tendencies, reads these later sections of the *Grammar* as little more than an "application" (166). My claim here finds additional support in Burke's *Permanence and Change* wherein he claims that we can "return through symbolism to a philosophy of *being.*"

14. Although he does not provide any detailed textual analysis for his conclusion, in an early review of the *Grammar* Abraham Kaplan suggests that Burke's "pentadic analyses" exceed the protocols articulated in the book. He writes, "For in fact the so-called internal transformations traced by Burke in motivational discourse are not strictly logical, but socio- and psycho-logical. The patterns of connection lie only in the extra-logical purport, and this must be dealt with in concrete empirical not abstract logical terms" (171).

15. When commenting on Burke's desire to be "systematic," Lentricchia notes that "[b]y rooting human motivation in an ontological principle of freedom which itself is situated outside the historical process . . . [Burke] establishes a point of view outside history from which to mediate (tame) the conflicting interpretations within it" (1983, 58). Lentricchia's reading of dramatism is, of course, informed by his interpretation of the action/motion differential and, thus, radically deviates from my own. It is important to note, however, that even Lentricchia detects the dehistoricizing tendency of the dramatistic method.

16. Both Francis Fergusson and John Crowe Ransom comment upon the dehistoricizing tendency of dramatistic analysis. As Ransom puts it, "In general, the pentad is not so dramatic in practice as its derivation promised. More often than not, the situation examined is not felt as drama; enactment upon a stage is not imaginable" (1969, 162).

3. *A Rhetoric of Motives*, or Toward an Ontology of the Social

1. Although she does not read in the *Rhetoric* an ontology of the social, it is quite interesting to note that in her book *Rhetoric and Criticism*, Marie Hochmuth Nichols argues that a discussion of identification as a process must start with a "metaphysics" or "ontology" of the subject. She writes, "[Burke] remarks that the [dramatistic] approach, instead of being *epistemological* and thus centering upon perception, knowledge, learning, etc., shall be an *ontological* one, thus centering upon the *substantiality* of the act" (89). Nichols's book was, of course, published some time before poststructuralism became the dominant intellectual trend in the United States.

2. Although, as I have stated, the dominant trend in contemporary Burkeian scholarship is to read the *Rhetoric* as epistemology, I should like to

point out an important exception. In his article "Under the Sign of (An)ni-hilation: Burke in the Age of Nuclear Destruction and Critical Deconstruc-tion," David Cratis Williams discusses Burke's "ontological loop" and places it in productive relation to Jacques Derrida's "ontodeconstruction."

3. I should note here that contemporary critics are not alone in assessing the *Rhetoric* as a predominantly epistemic enterprise. For example, in his article "Prolegomena to Kenneth Burke," Malcolm Cowley writes, "Hav-ing defined his terms in the first volume, Burke goes forward in the second to discuss language as the medium of human relations. 'Rhetoric,' in Burke's sense is a very broad term; he seems to define it—though never in ex-actly these words—as the study of the linguistic and symbolic means by which human beings try to influence one another" (249). In an early work, L. Virginia Holland also advocates such an assessment of the *Rhetoric:* "When language is viewed in its rhetorical dimension, the concern is with becoming aware of *how* one is *utilizing* his 'naming' process when one per-suades another, or identifies himself with another through the use of linguis-tic structure" (15).

4. Here I am consciously trying to make use of a notion of history Burke had expressed in *A Grammar of Motives* and, I might add, one in which post-structuralists find significant resources. Burke writes: "But can we bring ourselves to realize just how overwhelmingly much of what we mean by 'reality' has been built up for us through nothing but our symbol systems? Take away our books, and what little do we know about history, biography, even something so 'down to earth' as the relative position of seas and conti-nents? What is our 'reality' for today (beyond the paper-thin line of our own particular lives) but all this clutter of symbols about the past combined with whatever things we know mainly through maps, magazines, newspapers, and the like about the present? In school, as they go from class to class, stu-dents turn from one idiom to another. The various courses in the curriculum are in effect but so many different terminologies. And however important to us is the tiny sliver of reality each of us has experienced firsthand, the whole overall 'picture' is but a construct of our symbol systems. To meditate on this fact until one sees its full implications is much like peering over the edge of things into an ultimate abyss. And doubtless that's one reason why, though man is typically the symbol-using animal, he clings to a kind of naive ver-bal realism that refuses to realize the full extent of the role played by sym-bolicity in his notions of reality" (1966a, 5). Later in my analysis of the *Rhetoric* I try to push this notion of the "textuality" of history a bit further, arguing that one can read in the book the suggestion that the social is itself a *kind* of text.

5. It should be pointed out that Burke had established as early as *Counter-Statement* the biological, indeed ontological, rootedness of the so-cial. He writes, "Insofar as the neurological structure remains constant, there will be a corresponding constance in the devices by which sociality is maintained" (91). Such notation challenges further the argument that Burke's corpus can be read as a movement from epistemology to ontology.

6. Burke makes a parallel argument regarding the materialistic interpre-tation of these books. He argues that the materialistic interpretation per-

forms the same concealment, but on a different register. Thus I will not plot the movement of this latter argument, given that its logic corresponds to that of the former.

7. It should be noted that Burke uses the uppercase whenever naming the social.

8. By implication, the argument I propose here confounds an interpretation of Burke's work that understands him to have "st[ood] Marx on his head and restor[ed] the upturned Hegel" (Gusfield). Rather than arguing that "[i]t is not human existence that determines consciousness but consciousness that determines existence, or at least they are coequal" (36), I am trying to rethink the category "consciousness" itself as it figures in Burke's work, a rethinking that finds itself enabled by the suggestion that "consciousness" and "experience" are complicitous structures.

9. Recently a handful of critics have become interested in positing Burke's "metabiology" as the absolute point of departure for an understanding of Burke's theory of language. As Louis Gallo puts it in his article "Kenneth Burke: The Word and the World," "if there is to be a starting point from which Burke builds his entire philosophy, it is the human body" (39). It is my view that neither action nor motion can be understood as the absolute origin either of the emergence of the human being or of Burke's philosophy. It is the dialectical relation between them that constitutes the origin as such.

10. Thomas Kreilkamp's chapter entitled "Kenneth Burke and Thomas Schelling: Toward a Relevant Conceptual Structure" is a cogent articulation of the way in which Burke's work can be interpreted if his notion of motion is slighted: "[Burke's] emphasis on symbolic action leads him to develop a concept of identity which underscores our connections with each other, rather than our separateness" (186).

11. Jane Blankenship, like many other critics, acknowledges that " 'mystery' resides in the human condition from the moment we are born into this world [as] separate physiological organism[s]" (143). However, having acknowledged the divisiveness that is inherent in humans, she, like others, displaces such a notion and the implications it has for the economy of the social by arguing that "as 'bodies that learn language,' we have devised a peculiarly collective social nature by means of our symbol systems" (143–44). My objection to this position is made clear in the discussion that follows.

12. The claim that one can read in the *Rhetoric* an ontology of the social finds further justification if one breaks out of the book proper and moves to an outside that enables this new interior to be constituted: *A Grammar of Motives*. Such a move is not, I should point out, a step obliged by some newfangled strategy of reading. It is a critical move authorized by the *Rhetoric* itself: "To identify A with B is to make A 'consubstantial' with B. Accordingly, since our *Grammar of Motives* was constructed about 'substance' as key term, the related rhetoric selects its nearest equivalent in the areas of persuasion and dissuasion, communication and polemic" (545). Here warning signs are put up for the reader: one is not only expected to read carefully; one is also expected to have read. The reader is forewarned that the latter book builds upon, extends, and, I am arguing, productively confounds the former with the addition of an all-important c-o-n. Here Burke is extending

his thinking on the ontology of the act to include an ontology of acts: "A doctrine of *consubstantiality,* either explicit or implicit, may be necessary to any way of life. For substance, in the old philosophies, was an *act;* and a way of life is an *acting-together;* and in acting together, men have common sensations, concepts, images, ideas, attitudes that make them *consubstantial"* (545). That such relation obtains between the *Grammar* and the *Rhetoric* not only adds additional credence to my central thesis; it also makes problematic the notion that "one can begin anywhere" in the attempt to come to terms with Burke.

13. It is perhaps for this reason that Burke defines rhetoric as that which "is thus made from the fragments of dialectic" (699), a proposition seldom noted by critics and one that stands in interesting opposition to Aristotle's definition of rhetoric as "the counterpart of dialectic."

14. It should be noted that Burke mentions, but does not discuss at length, the nonunity of social relations in the *Grammar.* "Human relationships," he states, "must be *substantial,* related by the copulative, the 'is' of 'being' " (505). One must, of course, keep in mind the paradox of substance, which makes problematic the determination of the one.

15. In a book that seeks explicitly to "systematize [Burke's] view of rhetoric," L. Virginia Holland writes, "Burke envisions a society of the future in which communication approaches the ideal. As he sees it, no social system will have ideal communication unless it is based on a system of ideal co-operation" (9). I am arguing here that such ideal is a structural impossibility, a claim that finds support in Burke's extended discussion of "pure persuasion." As he puts it, " 'pure persuasion' is as biologically unfeasible as that moment when the irresistible force meets the immovable body" (818).

16. In his book *Realism and Relativism: A Perspective on Kenneth Burke,* Robert Heath puts us on the track of reading Burke's "we" as a catachresis when he writes, "[a] new, encompassing order is not necessarily true; its power would arise, not from its correspondence to reality, but from the fact that it is intersubjectively accepted and lived as though it were true" (109). Though I do not intend, in any way, to imply that Heath's reading of the relation between rhetoric and the social shares in the assumptions of my own essay, I am indebted to him for the above suggestion. In fact, my own reading of the *Rhetoric* could be read as a supplement (in the Derridean sense of the word) of Heath's.

17. In his article "Kenneth Burke's Comedy: The Multiplication of Perspectives," Wayne Booth offers another interpretation of the "we" in Burke's work. He states, "Any good—that is, useful—language will . . . remind us that we are not the independent, separate egos that some modernist views have claimed—rather, the so-called 'I' is merely a unique combination of partially conflicting 'corporate' 'we's' (and it is here that we find Burke's reason for avoiding the first-person singular)" (123–24). If Booth is merely suggesting that for Burke the category "I" is the Human Being whose subjectivity is shaped in part by a given set of historical (which is to say symbolic) influences, then it may be the case that our readings are different but nonetheless compatible. If, however, the intent is to suggest that Burke systematically questions the category "Man" (and one cannot be sure given that Booth

does not develop his reading), then our views radically oppose one another. On the project of rethinking "Man" as a sign to which there belongs an origin or a historical, cultural, or linguistic limit and its implications for the critique of humanism, see Jacques Derrida's "The Ends of Man" in *Margins of Philosophy.*

18. In a book that oftentimes domesticates the philosophies of both Heidegger and Burke in order to produce a line of continuity between the two thinkers, Samuel B. Southwell makes the following argument: in the work of Burke, "language . . . is not an a priori; it is not a fixed structure and it does not exist only within subjectivity. The phenomena it produces are 'noumena' partly concealed but also partly revealed. So far from being timeless, it creates time. Language opens to the world and history. What Burke describes are the structures of that opening." In seeming anticipation of the objections to his reading of Burke, Southwell notes that "[o]ur habits of mind tend instantly to reject the notion that the structure described in this way might be proposed as ontologically fundamental" (40). Though I have strong disagreements with many of Southwell's claims regarding the correspondence between "the central structures of the later Heidegger and of Burke," I do concur with him on the above point. However, I take it in a decidedly different direction.

19. Here I am drawing from the resources of the term *mode* as a transitive verb meaning to put into existence. See *Oxford English Dictionary.*

4. Further Speculations on the Dialectic: *The Rhetoric of Religion*

1. For representative examples see James Chesebro and Bernard Brock.

2. As I have already noted, in the introduction to the *Grammar* Burke writes, "In our original plans for this project, we had no notion of writing a 'Grammar' at all. We began with a theory of comedy, applied to a treatise on human relations. . . . There were other notes, concerned with modes of expression and appeal in the fine arts, and with purely psychological or psychoanalytic matters. These we classed under the heading of Symbolic" (xix). Although a manuscript of the *Symbolic of Motives* is unofficially in limited circulation, Burke has permitted neither its publication nor its citation.

3. Later in *The Rhetoric of Religion* Burke defines the supernatural as "duplicating the human socio-political order" (240).

4. In a note to the fourth analogy Burke explicitly declares a revision in his thinking has taken place. He writes, "There is a related puzzle of this sort: In my *Grammar of Motives* . . . I made much of a terministic pentad: *act, scene, agent, agency, purpose.* At first glance they all might look like quite 'positive' terms—and without thinking explicitly about the problem, I took them to be so. For they are not terms that readily imply logical opposites. But later I came to realize that, though they are not thus 'polar,' neither are they simply 'positive.' They are really *questions.* . . . Thus, they are really but a set of *blanks to be filled out.* They are an algebra, not an arithmetic"

(26). Burke's identifying the project with algebra rather than arithmetic is, of course, key: unlike arithmetic, algebra deals in wholly synchronic relations.

5. It should be noted that Nelson does, however, take this observation in a direction wholly different from the one argued for here. Indeed, he claims that in *The Rhetoric of Religion* and Burke's other later writings we are presented with "the undecidable subject of poststructuralism—a problematic but not dismissable site for discourse. It is with poststructuralism, then, in its more reflective, plural, and, at least with figures like Roland Barthes and Jacques Derrida, playful posing and problematizing of categories that Burke's work finds its true homology and its most fitting basis for comparison and contrast" (171).

6. In a most interesting article entitled "Kenneth Burke's Logology: A Mock Logomochy," Timothy C. Murray deconstructs "logological dramatism" and in the midst of so doing reads Burke's theory of naming and the principle of the negative as a system of "verbal displacement."

7. For representative sources on Burke and poststructuralism see, for example, Frank Lentricchia (1983), Cary Nelson, and Samuel B. Southwell. On the relation between Burke and Foucault see Carole Blair, "Kenneth Burke and Michel Foucault."

8. Here, however, I should like to mark a slight disagreement with Melia's thesis that the "qualitative algebra" of logology is "more or less implicit in dramatism" and "is made manifest" in *The Rhetoric of Religion* "as the dramatistic emphasis on temporal change surrenders to a logological drive toward atemporal permanence" (66). As I have already noted, both in the main text and in a note, Burke's text declares a decided shift from an arithmetic to an algebraic conception of the relation between constituent elements in a text. Thus I regard the conceptual movement from the *Grammar* to *The Rhetoric of Religion* in terms of a disjunctive synthesis rather than in terms of a developmental or coherent and evolutionary process.

9. I should like to point out that Freccero's essay is singular in terms of the history of criticism of *The Rhetoric of Religion: Studies in Logology* in that it performs a close reading of one of the chapters in the book.

10. Burke's notion of "second nature" finds its undeclared antecedent in Karl Marx. As Henri Lefebvre notes in his article "Toward a Leftist Cultural Politics: Remarks Occasioned by the Centenary of Marx's Death," "The new culture of the body is not constructed as a relation with primary nature but rather with a second nature. (I borrow these two terms from Marx, who did not develop them.) Primary nature includes the forest, the sea, the desert; second nature envelops the city and machines, but also the elaborated body, a 'worked' body that is inseparable from its urban setting and its urban ornamentation. Second nature has the same elements as primary nature, but it is developed as the product of human work" (82).

11. In his review of the *Rhetoric of Religion*, F. P. Dinneen argues on behalf of a similarity between Burke's conception of genre and that of V. Propp: "Like Burke, Propp finds a kind of determinism here: *if* this is a folk tale, it *must* select from among the elements he has described." However, Dinneen argues that "the determinism [Propp] finds derives not from *language*, but from the *literary type*" (189). My claim here, of course, is that such differ-

ence between Burke and Propp does not obtain. To the contrary, it is my suggestion that both Burke and Propp appeal ultimately neither to the synchronic relations of language nor to literary type, but to diachrony itself. My own discussion here is heavily indebted to Fredric Jameson's analysis of generic criticism in "Magical Narratives: On the Dialectical Use of Genre Criticism."

5. From Communicative Action to Rhetorical Invention

1. As Habermas puts it in his critique of Derrida: "[w]riting counts as the absolutely originary sign, abstracted from all pragmatic contexts of communication, independent of speaking and listening subjects" (1987, 178).

2. See, for example, John B. Thompson, Christopher Norris, Jane Flax, and Drucilla Cornell.

3. As Thomas Farrell points out, this may in fact be the skirting move Habermas makes: "To be fair, Habermas wants to allow that there may be illocutionary and perlocutionary aspects to the same act, but he then wishes us to move to the dominant overall type of utterance and decide what it is. In this categorical realm, as in so many others, the cognitive reasserts itself through several further controversial distinctions: for instance, the perlocutionary is always parasitic (a corrupt derivative) on the more basic illocutionary form, and the perlocutionary always requires that the speaker withhold his true aim in performing the utterance" (195).

Works Cited

Abbeele, Georges Van Den. Introduction. Miami Theory Collective. ix–xxvi.

Althusser, Louis. "Ideology and Ideological State Apparatuses (Notes Towards an Investigation)." *Lenin and Philosophy and Other Essays.* Trans. Ben Brewster. New York: Monthly Review Press, 1979. 127–86.

Anderson, Perry. *In the Tracks of Historical Materialism.* New York and London: Verso, 1983.

Biesecker, Barbara. "Coming to Terms with Recent Attempts to Write Women into the History of Rhetoric." *Philosophy and Rhetoric* 25 (1992): 110–30.

Blair, Carole. "Kenneth Burke and Michel Foucault." Speech Communication Association. New Orleans, 4 Nov. 1988.

Blankenship, Jane. " 'Magic' and 'Mystery' in the Works of Kenneth Burke." Simons and Melia 128–55.

Booth, Wayne. "Kenneth Burke's Comedy: The Multiplication of Perspectives." *Critical Understanding: The Powers and Limits of Pluralism.* Chicago: University of Chicago Press, 1979. 99–138.

——. "Kenneth Burke's Way of Knowing." *Critical Inquiry* 1 (1974–75): 1–22.

Brantlinger, Patrick. *Crusoe's Footprints: Cultural Studies in Britain and America.* New York and London: Routledge, 1990.

Brock, Bernard. "Epistemology and Ontology in Kenneth Burke's Dramatism." *Communication Quarterly* 33 (1985): 94–104.

Burke, Kenneth. *Counter-Statement.* 1931. Berkeley: University of California Press, 1968.

——. "Definition of Man." *Language as Symbolic Action: Essays on Life,*

Literature, and Method. Berkeley: University of California Press, 1966a.
3–24.

——. "Dramatism and Logology." *Communication Quarterly* 33 (1985):
89–93.

——. "A Dramatistic View of the Origins of Language." *Language as Symbolic Action: Essays on Life, Literature, and Method*. Berkeley: University
of California Press, 1966b. 419–79.

——. *A Grammar of Motives and A Rhetoric of Motives*. New York: Meridian, 1962.

——. *Permanence and Change: An Anatomy of Purpose*. 3d Edition.
Berkeley: University of California Press, 1984.

——. *The Rhetoric of Religion: Studies in Logology*. 1961. Berkeley: University of California Press, 1970.

Bygrave, Stephen. *Kenneth Burke: Rhetoric and Ideology*. New York and London: Routledge, 1993.

Calhoun, Craig, ed. *Habermas and the Public Sphere*. Cambridge and London: MIT Press, 1992.

Chesebro, James. "Epistemology and Ontology as Dialectical Modes in the
Writings of Kenneth Burke." *Communication Quarterly* 36 (1988): 175–91.

Cornell, Drucilla. *Transformations: Recollective Imagination and Sexual
Difference*. New York and London: Routledge, 1993.

Cowley, Malcolm. "Prolegomena to Kenneth Burke." Rueckert, *Critical Responses* 247–51.

Crusius, Timothy. "Kenneth Burke's *Auscultation*: A 'Destruction' of Marxist Dialectic and Rhetoric." *Rhetorica* 6 (Autumn 1988): 355–79.

de Man, Paul. "Genesis and Genealogy (Nietzsche)." *Allegories of Reading:
Figural Language in Rousseau, Nietzsche, Rilke, and Proust*. New Haven
and London: Yale University Press, 1979. 79–102.

Derrida, Jacques. "The Ends of Man." *Margins of Philosophy*. Trans. Alan
Bass. Chicago: University of Chicago Press, 1982a. 109–36.

——. "Form and Meaning: A Note on the Phenomenology of Language."
Margins of Philosophy. Trans. Alan Bass. Chicago: University of Chicago
Press, 1982b. 155–73.

——. *Of Grammatology*. Trans. Gayatri Chakravorty Spivak. Baltimore and
London: Johns Hopkins University Press, 1976.

——. "Positions: Interview with Jean-Louis Houdebine and Guy Scarpetta."
Positions. Trans. Alan Bass. Chicago: University of Chicago Press, 1981.
37–96.

——. "White Mythology: Metaphor in the Text of Philosophy." *Margins of
Philosophy*. Trans. Alan Bass. Chicago: University of Chicago Press, 1982c.
207–71.

Dinneen, F. P. "Review of *The Rhetoric of Religion*." *General Linguistics* 13
(1973): 176–95.

Donoghue, Denis. *Ferocious Alphabets*. New York: Columbia University
Press, 1984.

Duncan, Hugh Dalziel. "A Review of 'A Rhetoric of Motives.' " Rueckert,
Critical Responses 256–60.

Dupré, Louis. *Marx's Social Critique of Culture*. New Haven and London: Yale University Press, 1983.

Eley, Geoff. "Nations, Publics, and Political Cultures: Placing Habermas in the Nineteenth Century." Calhoun 289–339.

Farrell, Thomas B. *Norms of Rhetorical Culture*. New Haven and London: Yale University Press, 1993.

Feehan, Michael. "Oscillation as Assimilation: Burke's Latest Revisions." *PreText* 6 (1985): 319–27.

Fergusson, Francis. "Kenneth Burke's *A Grammar of Motives*." Rueckert, *Critical Responses* 173–81.

Fields, A. Belden. "In Defense of Political Economy and Systemic Analysis: A Critique of Prevailing Theoretical Approaches to New Social Movements." Nelson and Grossberg 141–56.

Fiordo, Richard. "Kenneth Burke's Semiotic." *Semiotica: Journal of the International Association for Semiotic Studies* 23 (1978): 53–75.

Fisher, Walter, and Wayne Brockriede. "Kenneth Burke's Realism." *Central States* 35 (1984): 35–42.

Flax, Jane. *Disputed Subjects: Essays on Psychoanalysis, Politics and Philosophy*. New York and London: Routledge, 1993.

Fraser, Nancy. "Rethinking the Public Sphere: A Contribution to the Critique of Actually Existing Democracy." *The Phantom Public Sphere*. Ed. Bruce Robbins. Minneapolis: University of Minnesota Press, 1993. 1–32.

Freccero, John. "Logology: Burke on St. Augustine." White and Brose 52–67.

Gallo, Louis. "Kenneth Burke: The Word and the World." *North Dakota Quarterly* 42.1 (1974): 33–45.

Garlitz, R. E. "The Sacrificial Word in Kenneth Burke's Logology." *Recherches Anglaises et Américaines* 12 (1979): 33–44.

Gusfield, Joseph R. "The Bridge Over Separated Lands: Kenneth Burke's Significance for the Study of Social Action." Simons and Melia 28–54.

Habermas, Jürgen. *Communication and the Evolution of Society*. Trans. Thomas McCarthy. Boston: Beacon, 1979a.

——. *The Philosophical Discourse of Modernity: Twelve Lectures*. Trans. Frederick Lawrence. Cambridge: MIT Press, 1987.

——. *Postmetaphysical Thinking: Philosophical Essays*. Trans. William Mark Hohengarten. Cambridge and London: MIT Press, 1992.

——. "Postscript to *Knowledge and Human Interests*." *Philosophy of Social Sciences* 3 (1973): 157–89.

——. *The Theory of Communicative Action: Volume One*. Trans. Thomas McCarthy. Boston: Beacon, 1984.

——. *Toward a Rational Society: Student Protest, Science, and Politics*. Trans. Jeremy J. Shapiro. Boston: Beacon, 1970a.

——. "Towards a Theory of Communicative Competence." *Recent Sociology*. Ed. H. P. Dreitzel. *Recent Sociology* 2 (New York 1970b). 130–48.

——. "What Is Universal Pragmatics?" *Communication and the Evolution of Society*. Trans. Thomas McCarthy. Boston: Beacon, 1979b. 1–68.

Hall, Stuart. *The Hard Road to Renewal: Thatcherism and the Crisis of the Left*. London and New York: Verso, 1988.

Heath, Robert. "Kenneth Burke on Form." *Quarterly Journal of Speech* 65 (1979): 392–404.

——. *Realism and Relativism: A Perspective on Kenneth Burke.* Macon, GA: Mercer University Press, 1986.

Hohengarten, William Mark. Translator's Introduction. Habermas, *Postmetaphysical Thinking* vii–xx.

Holland, L. Virginia. *Counterpoint: Kenneth Burke and Aristotle's Theories of Rhetoric* [sic]. New York: Philosophical Library, 1959.

Jameson, Fredric. "Magical Narratives: On the Dialectical Use of Genre Criticism." *The Political Unconscious: Narrative as a Socially Symbolic Act.* Ithaca: Cornell University Press, 1981. 103–50.

——. "The Symbolic Inference; or, Kenneth Burke and Ideological Analysis." White and Brose 68–91.

Jennerman, D. L. "Some Freudian Aspects of Burke's Aristotelian Poetics." *Recherches Anglaises et Américaines* 12 (1979): 65–81.

Kaplan, Abraham. "A Review of *A Grammar of Motives.*" Rueckert, *Critical Responses* 169–73.

Kreilkamp, Thomas. *The Corrosion of the Self: Society's Effects on People.* Irvington: New York University Press, 1976.

Laclau, Ernesto. "Community and Its Paradoxes: Richard Rorty's 'Liberal Utopia.' " Miami Theory Collective 83–98.

——. "Metaphor and Social Antagonisms." Nelson and Grossberg 249–57.

Laclau, Ernesto, and Chantal Mouffe. *Hegemony and Socialist Strategy: Towards a Radical Democratic Politics.* Trans. Winston Moore and Paul Cammack. London: Verso, 1985.

Lee, Benjamin. "Textuality, Mediation, and Public Discourse." Calhoun 402–18.

Lefebvre, Henri. "Toward a Leftist Cultural Politics: Remarks Occasioned by the Centenary of Marx's Death." Nelson and Grossberg 75–88.

Lentricchia, Frank. *Criticism and Social Change.* Chicago: University of Chicago Press, 1983.

——. "Discussion of Burke's Speech at the Congress, April 27, 1935." Simons and Melia 274–80.

——. "Reading History with Kenneth Burke." White and Brose 119–49.

Lyotard, Jean-François. *The Postmodern Condition: A Report on Knowledge.* Trans. Geoff Bennington and Brian Massumi. Minneapolis: University of Minnesota Press, 1984.

Mansbridge, Jane. "Feminism and Democracy." *The American Prospect* 1 (Spring 1990): 126–39.

Martin, Bill. *Matrix and Line: Derrida and the Possibilities of Postmodern Social Theory.* Albany: State University of New York Press, 1992.

McCarthy, Thomas. *The Critical Theory of Jürgen Habermas.* Cambridge and London: MIT Press, 1978.

Melia, Trevor. "Scientism and Dramatism: Some Quasi-Mathematical Motifs in the Work of Kenneth Burke." Simons and Melia 55–73.

Miami Theory Collective, eds. *Community at Loose Ends.* Minneapolis: University of Minnesota Press, 1991.

Murray, Timothy. "Kenneth Burke's Logology: A Mock Logomochy." *Glyph 2*. Baltimore: Johns Hopkins University Press, 1978. 144–61.

Nancy, Jean-Luc. *The Inoperative Community*. Ed. Peter Connor. Trans. Peter Connor, Lisa Garbus, Michael Holland, and Simona Sawhney. Minneapolis: University of Minnesota Press, 1991.

Neild, Elizabeth. "Kenneth Burke and Roland Barthes: Literature, Language and Society." *Recherches Anglaises et Américaines* 12 (1979): 98–108.

Nelson, Cary. "Writing as the Accomplice of Language: Kenneth Burke and Poststructuralism." Simons and Melia 156–73.

Nelson, Cary, and Lawrence Grossberg, eds. *Marxism and the Interpretation of Culture*. Urbana and Chicago: University of Illinois Press, 1988.

Nemerov, Howard. "Everything, Preferably All at Once: Coming to Terms with Kenneth Burke." *Sewanee Review* 79 (1971): 189–201.

Nichols, Marie Hochmuth. *Rhetoric and Criticism*. Baton Rouge: Louisiana State University Press, 1963.

Norris, Christopher. "Deconstruction, Postmodernism and Philosophy: Habermas on Derrida." *Derrida: A Critical Reader*. Ed. David Wood. Oxford and Cambridge: Blackwell, 1992. 167–92.

Oravec, Christine. "Kenneth Burke's Concept of Association and the Complexity of Identity." Simons and Melia 174–95.

Ortega y Gasset, José. *The Modern Theme*. Trans. James Cleugh. New York: Harper & Row, 1961.

Peters, John Durham. "Distrust of Representation: Habermas on the Public Sphere." *Media, Culture and Society* 15 (1993): 541–71.

Ransom, John Crowe. "Mr. Burke's Dialectic." Rueckert, *Critical Responses* 159–63.

Rueckert, William, ed. *Critical Responses to Kenneth Burke*. Minneapolis: University of Minnesota Press, 1969a.

——. *Kenneth Burke and the Drama of Human Relations*. Minneapolis: University of Minnesota Press, 1963.

——. "Kenneth Burke and Structuralism." *Shenandoah* 21 (1969b): 19–28.

——. "Rereading Kenneth Burke: Doctrine Without Dogma, Action With Passion." Simons and Melia 239–62.

——. "Some of the Many Kenneth Burkes." White and Brose 1–30.

Schrag, Calvin O. *The Resources of Rationality: A Response to the Postmodern Challenge*. Bloomington: Indiana University Press, 1992.

Searle, John R. *Speech Acts: An Essay in the Philosophy of Language*. Cambridge: Cambridge University Press, 1970.

Simons, Herbert W., and Trevor Melia, eds. *The Legacy of Kenneth Burke*. Madison: University of Wisconsin Press, 1989.

Southwell, Samuel B. *Kenneth Burke and Martin Heidegger: With a Note Against Deconstruction*. Gainesville: University of Florida Press, 1987.

Spivak, Gayatri Chakravorty. *In Other Worlds: Essays in Cultural Politics*. New York and London: Methuen, 1987.

——. Lectures on Marx. Seminar. University of Pittsburgh. Pittsburgh, August–December 1988.

——. Translator's Preface. Derrida, *Grammatology* ix–lxxxvii.

Stauffer, Donald A. "Salvation Through Semantics." Rueckert, *Critical Responses* 182–87.

Thompson, John B. *Critical Hermeneutics: A Study in the Thought of Paul Ricoeur and Jürgen Habermas.* Cambridge: Cambridge University Press, 1981.

Todorov, Tzvetan. *Theories of the Symbol.* Trans. Catherine Porter. Ithaca: Cornell University Press, 1982.

Vitanza, Victor. "A Mal-Lingering Thought (Tragic-Comedic) About KB's Visit." *PreText* 6 (1985): 163–67.

Wellek, Rene. "Kenneth Burke and Literary Criticism." *Sewanee Review* 79 (1971): 171–88.

White, Hayden, and Margaret Brose. *Representing Kenneth Burke.* Baltimore: Johns Hopkins University Press, 1982.

Williams, David Cratis. "Under the Sign of (An)nihilation: Burke in the Age of Nuclear Destruction and Critical Deconstruction." Simons and Melia 196–223.

Wood, Allen W. "Habermas' Defense of Rationalism." *New German Critique* 35 (1985): 145–64.

Index

Supernatural, 55, 56, 57
Symbolic action, 12, 24, 29, 45, 50, 58,
88, 96, 106 (n. 6), 107 (nn. 8, 10), 109
(n. 4)

Temporality, 56, 61, 71–73, 89, 101
Translation, 65

Trinity, 65
Truth, 80–82

Wellek, Rene, 104 (n. 3)
Williams, David, 109 (n. 2)
Wood, Allen W., 86

About the Series

STUDIES IN RHETORIC AND COMMUNICATION
General Editors:
E. Culpepper Clark, Raymie E. McKerrow, and David Zarefsky

The University of Alabama Press has established this series to pub-
lish major new works in the general area of rhetoric and communication, including books treating the symbolic manifestations of political discourse, argument as social knowledge, the impact of machine
technology on patterns of communication behavior, and other topics
related to the nature or impact of symbolic communication. We actively solicit studies involving historical, critical, or theoretical analyses of human discourse.

About the Author

Barbara A. Biesecker received her M.A. from Miami University in
Oxford, Ohio, and her Ph.D. from the University of Pittsburgh.